THE GiRLS
NEXT DOOR™

Paul Ruditis

SIMON SPOTLIGHT ENTERTAINMENT
New York London Toronto Sydney

Simon Spotlight Entertainment
A Division of Simon & Schuster, Inc.
1230 Avenue of the Americas
New York, NY 10020

First Simon Spotlight Entertainment hardcover edition
December 2008

SIMON SPOTLIGHT ENTERTAINMENT and colophon are
trademarks of Simon & Schuster, Inc.

For information about special discounts for bulk pur-
chases, please contact Simon & Schuster Special Sales
at 1-800-456-6798 or business@simonandschuster.com

Designed by Richard Oriolo

Manufactured in the United States of America

10 9 8 7 6 5 4 3 2 1

Library of Congress Cataloging-in-Publication Data is
available.

ISBN-13: 978-1-4165-9240-2
ISBN-10:   1-4165-9240-7

Contents

Welcome to our world! And thank you for following us on this crazy journey . . .

Three and a half years ago I could never have imagined that we would still be filming The Girls Next Door . . . yet at press time we will have finished a fifth season! Through my online fan club and MySpace, we have been able to get tons of feedback and questions from you guys. It was my mission to get some of the things you have been asking for compiled into book form. From Bridget's favorite recipes to my makeup tips to Kendra's signature meal at Olive Garden, you will find it all here.

Thanks for sticking with us!

Love,

Holly Madison

Hey, Guys!

It is finally here—the book we have been talking about for so long now!

I know so many of you have wanted this to happen for a really long time. You all have been so supportive. I appreciate your patience, enthusiasm, and loyalty! Your interest and fascination with our lifestyle are why we are able to have the highest-rated show on E!—and to do fun projects like this book.

This book is written for you, our fans, and we tried to fill it with information on everything about our lifestyles, from hair, makeup, and style tips to hosting theme parties!

I have also tried to answer some of the burning questions that I get asked a lot, such as, "What kind of dog is Wednesday?" and "Where did I get Gizmo's cat tree?", not to mention the requests I get for the recipe for my parents' now-famous cottage cheese dip!

I hope you enjoy this book, but most of all, I hope it works as a guide to inspire you to follow your dreams, be happy, and live the life that you want to live.

Happy reading!

XOXO,

Bridget Marquardt

Hey!

You think you know a lot about Holly, Bridget, and me from watching our show? Well, you do! But now we're getting even more personal, with a whole book devoted to our lives at the Playboy Mansion. It's loaded with friends, favorite moments, and some of the stuff we've learned over the years, like posing tips and even an etiquette lesson, K-dub style! It's like our own little scrapbook that we get to share with you.

Hef has given me such a great opportunity to try new things and find out who I am. And this book is like a walk down memory lane, with hot pictures on every page. So sit back, relax, and spend some time with The Girls Next Door!

Love ya!

Kendra Wilkinson xoxo

For decades it has been seen as the ultimate bachelor pad, a place where swinging single men can enjoy hedonistic pleasures with a gaggle of beauties. But the Playboy Mansion—or Playboy Mansion West, to use its proper name—has always been more than simply the home of Hugh M. Hefner. It has provided shelter for the women in his life, each of whom brings her own influence to the Playboy lifestyle. With the premiere of the hit reality show on the E! network, the public has truly become aware of what life is like behind the Mansion's gates, not from the perspective of the man of the house, but from the viewpoints of The Girls Next Door.

Our Life with Hef

THE STORY OF *The Girls Next Door*, however, does begin with the legendary Hugh Hefner, better known as Hef. For decades, Hef was the living embodiment of the Playboy philosophy of sexuality that began with the launch of his magazine in 1953 and grew into a vast empire that included television, licensing, and club casinos. Though *Playboy* was relatively mild in comparison to the imitators that followed, Hef grew accustomed to his role of shocking the world with every move he made. Little seemed more outrageous than when he settled down and married Kimberley Conrad in the eighties. Their union lasted only a decade, but the two never formally divorced. In 1999, when they separated, Hef was not looking forward to life as a bachelor again, particularly after a friend warned him that at their age "the women at the clubs look right through you." **"THE NOTION OF** going back to my previous life at that age seemed unthinkable," Hef says. But with those words of warning echoing in his mind, he took his first tentative steps back into the dating pool. He learned quickly that his fears were unfounded. "What I discovered was that, literally, a whole generation had grown up and was waiting for me to come out and play. Both boys and girls. I was dating Playmates from the get-go, and other beautiful ladies, and age seemed to have absolutely no meaning. All of a sudden I was not feeling old. I was feeling much younger. A decade-plus later, I was feeling much younger than I had in the late eighties." **HIS NEW LOVE** life began at the young age of

seventy-three when he met an actress named Brande Roderick, and it quickly took an unexpected turn when Hef was out clubbing one night. "I looked across the room and there was a pair of stunning identical twins. I managed to lure them over to my table and ordered them a drink." The trio started talking. Hef learned that their names were Sandy and Mandy Bentley and that they were from his hometown, Chicago. They hit it off as the evening progressed, though it didn't end up the way Hef thought it would. "I thought they were going home with me that night, but they went to the bathroom, and when I turned around they were gone. Then, in the next month, I literally tracked them down. And that, in itself, was quite remarkable." ❧ **ONCE HE FOUND** the Bentley twins, Hef began dating Sandy, Mandy, and Brande, "Which sounds like bad fiction, but a lot of fun," he admits. When Brande was cast in *Baywatch*, which filmed in Hawaii, that relationship ended. But the idea of dating several girls at the same time seemed natural to Hef at that point. "So I started looking at other girls and other possibilities and that turned, in time, to seven girlfriends at one point. Some of those times were good and some of them were tumultuous." ❧ **IN AND AMONG** those various relationship incarnations, Hef's entourage of females welcomed a new face in the form of Holly Madison. "I got invited with a bunch of other Hawaiian Tropic girls to come to a party," Holly recalls. Her introduction to the Mansion came during the Midsummer Night's Dream party. "It was just beautiful. The backyard was set up in such a wonderful way. It was a really fun night." And on that night, she met the man who would become her "Puffin," though their initial hello was brief. ❧ **HOLLY THEN CAME** back to the Mansion's Sunday Fun in the Sun pool parties, held every weekend in the warmer months. "Everybody here was so nice. There's just a real feeling of family and community, with all of Hef's friends," she says. She was welcomed into that family and became a regular visitor to the Mansion, eventually letting Hef know of her interest in dating him. "In most cases in my life, I've picked the girl," Hef admits. "I think Holly picked me. . . . Because she waited to let me know that she was interested. She gave me a little picture of her, a sexy picture of her. I just thought that she was interested in posing for the magazine. So I wasn't paying a lot of attention. But eventually she said something to get my interest and I invited her out with the group and we were together that night." Holly moved in two days later. ❧ **WHILE HOLLY MADE** her way through the hierarchy of girlfriends, another girl from a small town caught Hef's eye. Bridget Marquardt had dreamed of posing for *Playboy* her entire life. She finally seized her opportunity when she saw an advertisement for the Millennium Playmate Search. Bridget attended a casting call in San Francisco and was one of the lucky few selected to visit Los Angeles to test for the magazine. Though she ultimately wasn't chosen to appear, Bridget did not give up on her lifelong dream, finding a way back to the Mansion in the most unlikely of places. "A friend of mine was seeing a plastic surgeon to get her boobs done," Bridget recalls. "He was going to the Playboy Mansion for the Midsummer party and I asked him, 'How can I get to do that?' He told me that I just had to submit a picture." Bridget and her friend did just that. It was so last-minute that she had to overnight the photo to make the cut. She made it in time and received an invitation, though her friend

did not. "So, by myself," she says, "I went to the Midsummer Night's Dream party." 🐰 **WHILE AT THE** party, Bridget met some of Hef's close friends and developed her own friendship with them. When she finally decided to move to L.A. full-time a few months later, Bridget contacted those friends and re-connected, wrangling an immediate invitation as a guest to dinner at the Mansion. "They brought me here," she recalls, "and I got to know people. Eventually I was invited on my own to the dinners, then to Sunday Fun in the Sun, where I made friends with the girls. And then one day, Hef was like, 'Hey, do you want to come out with us?'" 🐰 **HOLLY AND BRIDGET** were still two faces in a group, but they were both growing closer to Hef when the third member of the trio came along. The story of Hef stumbling across Kendra's photo in the color printer is now *Girls Next Door* legend. It was a random sighting that sent the Mansion staff scrambling to find out the identity of the mysterious girl who was being considered for one of the Painted Ladies at Hef's upcoming birthday. Phone calls were made and a meeting was arranged when Kendra came to the Mansion for the party. 🐰 **"I MET HIM** at his seventy-eighth birthday party," Kendra recalls. "And then everything just happened. He asked me to keep coming back every weekend. But I didn't want to move in so fast. I never was a girlie girl. I was looking at these girls and thinking, 'Do I have to start looking like that?' I didn't really get it." 🐰 **HEF ARRANGED FOR** a car to pick up Kendra and drive her from San Diego to the L.A. Mansion every weekend. During that time, Kendra learned that Hef liked her for exactly who she was and didn't want her to change a thing. Other changes had to be made, though, particularly with the ever-shifting number of girlfriends. **"A MOMENT CAME,"** Hef recalls somewhat wistfully, "when the relationships were not working well. The motivations for all the girls being here were varied. Some of them were sincere. Some of them were here for publicity. Some of them were here for the money." But when Kendra came along, Hef felt it was time to, in his words, "Thin the herd, to reduce the number of girls and put the emphasis on quality rather than quantity. So I took those steps and said pleasant good-byes to the other girls." 🐰 **THE NEW HIERARCHY** became Holly as the first girlfriend, with Bridget and Kendra also sharing in Hef's affections. It's a grouping that you either understand or don't, but it works for them, and especially for Hef. "People ask me, 'How do you get along with three girlfriends?' And I say, 'Hey, it is easier than getting along with one wife. It's not numbers—it's who they are.' Despite the age disparity, against all logic, Holly is the best relationship I've ever had. We have remarkably common interests. It is the living evidence that age is just a number. If you are healthy, you really don't know how old you are."

KENDRA: Hef is everything. I said on the show the other day that Hef should have his own holiday, like Valentine's Day. Hef should have his own Hef Day. He's the greatest guy in the world. You always hear guys say that they want to be Hugh Hefner. Now, come on! If they really knew Hugh Hefner . . . if they really knew how romantic he is, how he treats everyone around him, and how hard he works every day . . . Those guys want to live his life, but they will never compare. It makes me so mad. They don't see Hef for who he is. They just see the girls around him.

BRIDGET: Hef is charismatic and a gentleman. He's a little kid at heart, which makes him really fun. He's also inspirational because of all that he's accomplished and everything that he's had to put up with, and yet he's still so positive and doesn't care what people think. He's living the lifestyle he wants to live. And now, because he does that, he's iconic. People want to be like him, and people worship the lifestyle he has. He can walk down the hall to work in his pajamas every day, and that's socially acceptable.

HOLLY: Hef is a world unto himself. He's created his own thing and made it into such a success. He's got this whole community around him that just adores him. And he's so busy. He's got so much work keeping him occupied. Right now he's working on a screenplay and editing several books in addition to all he does for the magazine. It's crazy the stuff that fills up his life. But still we have time to watch movies together and play games. I always like it when he comes outside and spends time with the animals. He's an amazing person who is really sweet and really sensitive. He is one of the greatest influences in my life and will always be one of my best friends.

Nothing in the childhood of the girl born Holly Cullen in Astoria, Oregon, who

would become Holly Madison, could have prepared her for life at the Playboy

Mansion or for being on the arm of one of the most famous men in the world.

Her family moved from Oregon when she was two, and her younger years were spent in a small town in Alaska, which did have its benefits. "It was a really good place to grow up because

of the lifestyle. It was very outdoorsy and low-tech. I was always playing outside

and using my imagination," she remembers fondly. "Things emphasized today in

children's lives, especially in most of America, are materialism and growing up

too fast. So I was lucky."

With a father in the timber industry, Holly moved around a lot during her tween and teen years, settling back in Oregon, though never in one place for very long. This was particularly difficult for the girl who freely admits that she is

"a shy person." Making new friends wherever she moved was a daunting task. She did find a place to fit in when she was a cheerleader for the Lions of St. Helen's High School, but after graduation she realized that Los Angeles was her true destination—not because of her dreams of the Playboy Mansion, but because of her love for another famous place. 🐰 "My family and I would always vacation here every year," she recalls of her childhood visits to Southern California. "We'd go to Anaheim and to Disneyland. I feel like that's another hometown to me. I just always loved Los Angeles. I love the weather. I love the attitude people have. They have an attitude like anything is possible, which people do not necessarily have in the rest of the country or the world. You can't always dream big in other places and have people appreciate that or humor it. But here you can do anything." 🐰 Though Disney was—and is—her passion, Holly found work at the Santa Monica Hooters and as a Hawaiian Tropic girl, which eventually led her to the Mansion and Hugh Hefner. And after a brief pursuit, she found her Prince Charming when Hef asked her out on their first date. "We went to a club called Las Palmas in Hollywood," she recalls, "which was really, really hot at the time. I don't feel like there's been a club that good in L.A. since then. We went with something like ten other girls and we just danced all night and had a really good time." 🐰 She'd be the first to

admit that hers isn't exactly a Cinderella story, but it works for her. Initially, though, the

numbers didn't work; being one in a sea of girlfriends was not her ambition. "I was here

for maybe two and a half years before it got cut down, but it was long overdue," she

says. And now the group has been culled down to three very close friends. Though Holly

admits that she would have liked to have her "Puffin" all to herself, she is happy that

the foursome has become a happy family and that she can share their life with the world

through *The Girls Next Door.*

Now that your *show is so successful*, do you have any control over what we see on it?

At first we were not allowed to see a rough cut because nobody wanted to hear what we thought. Nobody really wanted our opinions. Now **WE DO GET TO SEE** the rough cuts and can make some suggestions. We respect the fact that the producers need to make a show out of what we do, though. So unless something is really way off-base, it's rare that we have a complaint or say "this needs to be changed." It almost never happens. We're not going to make a fuss out of something petty and be the boy who cried wolf. We only want to tell the producers if something's not right, or if we think they're not getting the full story and maybe didn't see all the footage.

Hef, Holly, Bridget and Kendra

How is life with cameras following you around?

Having the cameras around is pretty easy, but there are certain things I try to avoid. I prefer that they don't shoot in my room too much, partly because Hef doesn't want them in there, in his side of the room. He also doesn't want them in my side of the room if he's changing or getting ready or using the restroom, obviously. My part of the room is so packed and so messy it's impossible for anybody to navigate, let alone with a big camera. My dogs also freak out on the camerapeople. They're constantly yapping. So I try not to film anything in my room if I can help it.

The one thing that's irritating about filming isn't the cameras; it's the microphones, and having to stop what we're doing to get miked. It's the poor sound guy who we complain about, though it's not his fault. He's always saying, "Hey, can you move your microphone? Your necklace is hitting it." It stops *everything*, but they have to be able to hear us. Still, everybody asks about the cameras. IT'S NOT THE CAMERAS—IT'S THE MICROPHONES.

I know that one of the things you are most proud of is your work with Playboy on Operation Playmate. Tell us a little about that.

Operation Playmate is a service we have where we send signed headshots to the guys who are fighting overseas to boost their morale. The e-mail address is **operation_playmate@playboy.com**. People can write in and send me their soldier's mailing address—either an APO or an FPO—and I will have the girls sign headshots and send the soldier a selection.

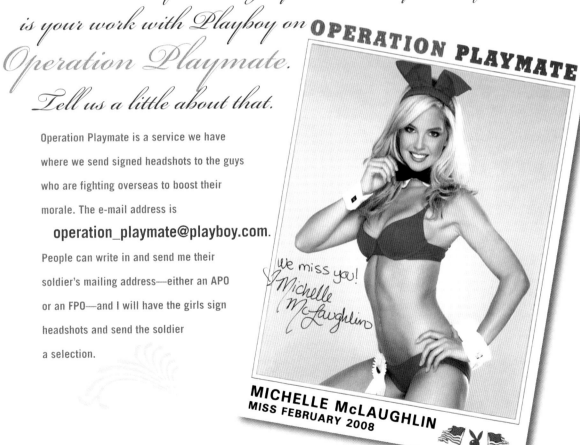

OPERATION PLAYMATE

we miss you!
Michelle McLaughlin

MICHELLE McLAUGHLIN
MISS FEBRUARY 2008

Being one of Hef's girlfriends seems to have given you many opportunities to branch out and try new things, like acting. Of those experiences, which have been your most memorable?

I think my favorite show that I was on was *Curb Your Enthusiasm*. It's a really good show and I was excited to be on. It was really fun to do a scene with Larry David because it was all improvisational. So I loved that. And I loved doing *The House Bunny* with Anna Faris. The script was funny and the art direction was really cute. I felt like the movie was kind of based on our show.

And of course being at the Mansion gave you the chance to meet the man who created one of your favorite films, Star Wars.

Yeah. George Lucas came to one of our New Year's parties. Sara Underwood—the 2007 Playmate of the Year—and I love the same movies. We're both really big into *Star Wars* and *Labyrinth* and *Indiana Jones*. I told Sara, "I dare you to go say hi to George Lucas." So she goes over to him and says, "Holly dared me to come say hi to you." And then he looked really annoyed and turned to his date and said something. Then Sara left and I was so embarrassed. Some meeting.

Your feelings toward Playboy are pretty clear, considering you had the logo tattooed on your body. How did that come about?

I got my Bunny tattoo not long after I moved into the Mansion. I was just hanging out with my friend Ashley and decided I wanted to get a TATTOO, and I wanted it to be something cute. I don't know; I guess I just had a wild hare up my ass. Wait. I can't believe I just said that.

Slam Book of Holly Madison

As a child, what did you want to be when you grew up?

To be an author, or to work for Disney.

Today, what do you want to be when you grow up?

I'm a photo editor, and that's what I want to be.

What are your turn-ons and turnoffs?

My turn-ons are creative genius, dark hair, and ambition. My turnoffs are slow walkers, bad Photoshop, and pussies who won't ride roller coasters.

Who was the first boy you kissed?

Some guy in junior high. And he slipped me the tongue. I was really grossed out because I wasn't expecting it.

What was your best Halloween costume as a child?

I was She-Ra in first grade. It was a homemade costume, but it rocked because the store-bought ones were lame and looked nothing like She-Ra's actual outfit.

What was the name of your childhood pet?

I had a black cat named Jenny, and we had an Afghan dog named Ginger.

What's your sign? Capricorn.

What is your favorite . . . *Food?* Dill pickles.   *Color?* Red, black, and white.   *Number?* Twenty-three.

Movie? I love movies! My list includes A Christmas Story, Once Upon a Time in America, The Doors, The Goonies, Return of the Jedi, Fear and Loathing in Las Vegas, To Catch a Thief, Strangers on a Train, Marie Antoinette, Moulin Rouge!, Chicago, and anything with Marilyn Monroe, Jean Harlow, or Grace Kelly.

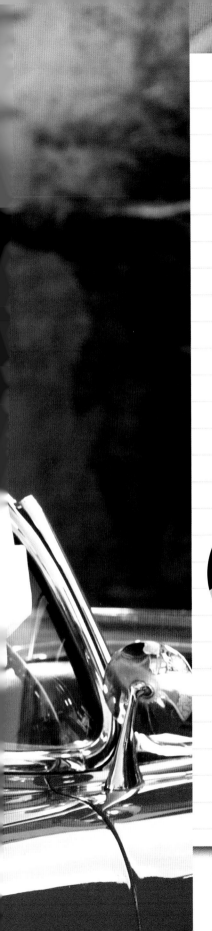

Movie that Hef introduced you to? *City Lights,* with Charlie Chaplin.

Disney character? *Belle from Beauty and the Beast.*

TV show? *Criss Angel Mindfreak.*

Book? *Marilyn Monroe: The Biography,* by Donald Spoto. It's the best Marilyn Monroe book.

Singer/Band? *Billy Joel, Frank Sinatra, KISS, Sublime, Nirvana, Blondie, Rob Zombie, Mötley Crüe, AFI, and the Doors.*

Playmate? *Heather Kozar, 1999 Playmate of the Year. She looks like Marilyn Monroe, but hotter. I wanted to be her when I grew up.*

A Day in the Life of
Holly Madison

7:30 Roll out of bed . . . I don't wanna get up! Shower, get dressed, order breakfast.

8:00 Take the dogs outside. Bring them back into the Mediterranean Room for breakfast.

8:30 Throw on a microphone for *The Girls Next Door* crew and leave for the studio with Kayla, the new Playmate we are shooting today. A cameraman climbs into the backseat and asks me to turn off the radio.

8:45 Stop at Starbucks and grab a venti Iced Caffé Americano.

9:00 Arrive at the studio. Hang out in the makeup room with Kayla and Sara, the makeup artist.

9:15 Do crunches.

9:20 Check e-mail and MySpace comments and fan club.

10:10 Send off the last mock-ups for the 2009 *Girls Next Door* calendar.

10:20 Drop off Playmate promo shots.

10:30 Supervise Kayla's Centerfold shoot. I pick four pictures to send home to Hef as samples.

12:00 Lunch! I have California rolls.

1:00 Still awaiting Hef's reaction to the Centerfold. I dress up in an outrageous outfit from our wardrobe room and clown around with my co-workers.

2:30 Post a blog on my fan club about how bored I am waiting for the phone call!

3:00 Hef calls and tells me the Centerfold is approved! I go back on set to do the lingerie version of the Centerfold.

4:00 Grab a margarita. It's a fellow employee's last day, so we're partying.

4:04 Call the Mansion to make sure the dogs have been fed.

5:00 Drive home with Kayla.

6:00 French tutor meets me at the Mansion.

7:30 Say au revoir to my French tutor. Join Bridget, Cristal, and Kayla to go to a Paige Jeans party on Robertson.

9:00 Walk the dogs after returning home.

9:15 Get into pj's. Order dinner and watch a *Columbo* mystery with Puffin. I have whole-wheat angel-hair pasta with marinara sauce, broccoli, and ice water for dinner.

Anything I do later is not fit to print.

Little Bridget Sandmeier did not dream of being a Disney Princess. Her lifelong ambition stemmed from a different view of female perfection and was formed at a very young age when she stumbled across her father's copy of *Playboy*. Bridget was entranced by the beautiful women in the magazine, which continued to inspire her throughout her teen years. *Bridget's* parents were together off and on during her childhood and separated permanently when she was nine. Since her father was a truck driver, it was often just Bridget, her brother, and their mom around the house. But she did hail from a very large, very loving family with many aunts, uncles, and cousins. Her grandmother often watched her when her mom worked the late shift at the hospital. Her mom eventually remarried and the family—which soon welcomed a baby sister into the mix— moved out to the country. There, Bridget enjoyed a new life among the horses and cows, joined the 4-H and raised a show rabbit of her own.

Even within her close family, Bridget embraced her individuality. "My mom was very supportive of me being independent and a little bit different. I think that makes me who I am today. I feel like I'm a stronger person because of that." That strength saw her through school and the completion of her master's degree in communications. She was content, but at the same time she felt like there was something more. "I would wake up in the middle of the night feeling like something was missing in my life, that there was something bigger in life for me." *Although* her first attempt to contact *Playboy* did not even net a reply ("I figured it was because I was seventeen and they didn't want to respond"), fate intervened when someone in her circle later sent an issue of the magazine to her house as a joke. It just so happened to have an advertisement for the magazine's Millennium Playmate Search. She dialed the number in the ad and made an appointment for the casting call. It was something she'd dreamed of almost her entire life, but she still wasn't quite prepared for the reality. She recalls the moment the photographer came out and made it clear to all the girls that he was going to ask them to take their tops off for the test photo. "This had never occurred to me before," she says, laughing. "They said bikinis and heels. I figured that's what we were going to take pictures in. I never imagined that they might actually ask us to take them *off*." Though she was free not to disrobe, Bridget screwed up her courage and removed her top when her turn came. *Apparently* the editors at *Playboy* liked what they saw because she got the call to come to L.A. for a test. "I was freaking out," she admits. "It was the most exciting moment of my life." Bridget went to L.A. for her test and met Hugh Hefner briefly, then returned home to Northern California, where the waiting game began. "It took a year and a half for me to find out that I didn't get it," she explains. Several calls to inquire were met with the standard response that until she heard a definitive answer, she was still in consideration. "But then I got a letter in the mail. It said, 'Thank you so much for your interest in being a Playmate. As you know, we can pick only twelve girls. Although you are very beautiful, you didn't make the cut.' I was devastated. I was crying. I was so upset."

But that was not the end of her Playmate ambitions. Still feeling that something was missing, Bridget packed her bags and moved to L.A. She became a Mansion regular before moving in for a permanent stay and eventually seeing her *Playboy* dreams come true.

Before we get to anything else, please take a moment to answer, once and for all, the top two questions you always get asked:

What kind of dog is Wednesday? She is a miniature Pekingese, also known as a **SLEEVE PEKINGESE** because the Chinese used to wear them in their sleeves when they were the dogs of royalty in China.
Where did you get Gizmo's cat tree? Although lots of pet stores sell them, I see them all the time on Ventura Boulevard in the valley. I got it at a pet store that I don't think is even there anymore. It was on La Brea and it was called For Pets Only. Gizmo loves her cat tree. That is her home.

One of your most emotional moments on the show was when you had to leave your first Playboy photo shoot early because you had a final exam. With all that going on, how did you do on the test?

I got an A! I got an A in the whole class. It was stressful. I did not want to miss out on any part of the photo shoot, and yet I'd done the whole semester of this class and I just couldn't miss the final. School's very important to me as well. So it was a very difficult day and a difficult decision to make. I was hoping that something would give—either we could finish the pictorial on another day or my teacher would let me finish the final on another day. It just didn't happen, and I had to go. Thankfully, it all worked out.

Why haven't you completed the course for your paranormal investigator's license?

Honestly, I was more interested in learning the stuff than in the actual certificate. I was full-on planning to complete the certificate. My paper was going to be on the Mansion, but when I started getting all the information, I was thinking, "This is a bigger story than just a paper. Maybe a book." I never really cared about the actual certificate. It was just kind of a fun project to work on. I loved learning all about the different instruments and how to conduct a proper investigation. The right things to do. The wrong things to do. Who cares about the certificate? What am I going to do, hang it on the wall?

You seem to take party themes very seriously.

To me, life is about enjoying every moment and making the most out of every occasion and every *thing*. That means theme-ing it all out as much as you can and as much as you want to.

Slam Book of Bridget Marquardt

Bridget's Disclaimer #1:

I'm so bad at favorites because I could say a favorite right now and later today I'll be like, "No, *that* was my favorite. Damn!" Or tomorrow I'll see something else and go, "Oh, that's my favorite now." But I'll try my best . . .

I think everyone knows the answer to this one, but, as a child, what did you want to be when you grew up?

I wanted to be in *Playboy*. It wasn't necessarily a career ambition, although it is a career in a lot of ways. But I never really thought of it as a *career* career. It was just what I aspired to be.

Today, what do you want to be when you grow up?

I definitely want to host my own television show. Ideally, it would be a travel show where I would go to different cities and talk about the coolest, quirkiest, and neatest things to do there.

What are your turn-ons and turnoffs?

My turn-ons are a handyman who can get the job done, ambition and motivation, and manners. My turnoffs are smoking, tardiness, negativity, and rude and selfish people.

Who was the first boy you kissed?

Well, if you count Spin the Bottle and a quick peck on the cheek, his name was Tommy. But my first real kiss, where I was actually into it, his name was Ernie. I was a late bloomer because I was, like, sixteen at the time. I was very, very, very shy.

What was your best Halloween costume as a child?

When I was really little, my mom dressed me as Marilyn Monroe and I thought I was really cute. She put my dad's socks in the boobs, did my hair up all curly, gave me a mole and the full makeup. I thought I was so hot and sexy, and I was like five.

What was the name of your childhood pet?

I was in 4-H, which is where students learn how to raise pets and to show them. So I raised a rabbit named Kissy. She was a miniature Netherland Dwarf, and she was a show rabbit.

What's your sign? Libra.

What is your favorite . . .

Food? Pizza. **Color?** Black, red, and blue. Yellow's always fun.

Number? Growing up it was sixteen. It was just a sweet, cute number. But then I got my edgy side and thirteen became my favorite number. Everyone else thinks it's bad luck, but I think it's good luck. I'm still kind of stuck on thirteen.

Movie?

The Orphanage or El Orfanato, The Exorcist, The Goonies, The Virgin Suicides, The Cat's Meow, and the new Marie Antoinette.

Movie that Hef introduced you to? The Thin Man series.

TV show? Ghost Hunters on the Sci-Fi channel and Ace of Cakes on the Food Network.

Book? Dr. Seuss's Oh the Places You'll Go.

Singer/Band? AC-DC.

Playmate? It's a toss-up between 2000 Playmate of the Year Jodi Ann Paterson and 1998 Playmate of the Year Karen McDougal.

A Day in the Life of
Bridget Marquardt

BRIDGET'S DISCLAIMER #2: First of all, let me start off by saying there is no such thing as a typical day for me. Even as I write this itinerary, I'm thinking, "It didn't happen this way today or yesterday, and it isn't going to go like this tomorrow." My life is constantly changing and evolving, with different priorities, responsibilities, and opportunities posed each day. This is the type of schedule I would shoot for if a day arrived in which I had no major obligations.

8:30 Wake up.

8:45 Take Wednesday outside.

9:00 Order coffee and Wednesday's breakfast.

9:10 Do Wednesday's tricks, feed her breakfast.

9:15 Answer e-mails, return phone calls, make daily to-do list.

9:45 Brush my teeth, wash my face.

10:00 Go down to office and talk to Mary.

10:30 Work out: sometimes in the gym at the Mansion, sometimes a hike, sometimes a run on the beach, and sometimes trapeze class.

On Thursdays at ten A.M. I have my live Web chat on my Web site: www.bridgetmarquardt.com.

On Fridays at ten A.M. I have *The Bridget & Wednesday Friday Show* on Playboy Radio/Sirius 198.

11:45 Shower.

12:00 Hair.

12:15 Makeup.

12:30 Get dressed.

12:45 Walk Wednesday.

1:00 Lunch time! I run back to the Mansion, hit up a fast-food place, or have a nice lunch with a friend, depending on my mood and how busy the day is.

1:30 Run errands. They vary depending on what is going on . . . shopping for upcoming parties or events, attending interviews or meetings for upcoming projects, or just boring stuff like the bank, car wash, etc.

4:30 Return home, pop down to the office and see what is going on, play with Wednesday and Gizmo.

5:00 Call Mom.

5:15 Walk Wednesday.

5:30 Check my e-mail again.

6:00 Get ready to go out to dinner with either all the girls and Hef or just the girls, depending on the night.

If it is a Friday, Saturday, or Sunday night, we have buffet dinner from five-thirty to seven, and then a movie at seven P.M.

7:30 Meet down in the dining room.

7:45 Leave for dinner.

10:00 Back home.

10:15 Walk Wednesday.

10:30 Wash my face, brush my teeth, put on my pj's.

10:45 Check e-mail again.

11:00 Get in bed, snuggle with Wednesday and Gizmo, watch TV, search the Web, or read until I get sleepy. I usually fall asleep sometime between eleven-thirty P.M and one A.M.

Kendra Wilkinson

"EVERYTHING JUST HAPPENED AFTER I GOT MY BOOBS DONE," KENDRA REVEALS in one of her patented moments of honesty. "Like I said on the show, and I'm not joking when I say that. I don't even know why I got my boobs done, because that wasn't really me. Getting my boobs done, like, *come on*. That so wasn't me." ✳ **NOT THAT KENDRA** is advocating plastic surgery as a cure-all for your problems—that would be the last thing the free-spirited tomboy would do. And it certainly was not the answer to her problems. Raised by a single mother after her father left when she was four, Kendra did not have an easy life. She freely admits that she didn't make life any easier for the mother who raised her. Kendra left home in her teens and went through what can euphemistically be called a "dark period." But, like the fighters she enjoys watching on Fight Night,

Kendra battled her demons and came out the other side stronger . . . and blonder. ☀ **IT WAS AFTER** she got her life back on track and made some out-of-character changes that the most unexpected thing happened. "I was going with my boys to this car show," she explains, "and someone asked me to pose in front of a bike for some pictures. I was like, 'Hell no! I don't want to do it. That's not me.'" But her friends convinced her it could be fun. "Next thing you know, I have a business card in my hand and a guy asking if I've ever done a photo shoot." And thus a modeling career was born. ☀ **KENDRA POSED FOR** a couple of photo shoots, one of which was put up on a Web page that was seen by Mark Frazier, the artist who creates the Painted Ladies for Hugh Hefner's parties. Mark contacted Kendra to ask her if she'd consider allowing him to submit her picture for consideration to be a Painted Lady at Mr. Hefner's upcoming birthday party. "I thought it was a little joke," Kendra said. "So I said, 'Sure, do it. See what happens.'" We all know what happened next. ☀ **"I GET OUT** of the shower and I'm all wet and stuff, and there's a call from the 310 [area code]," Kendra recalls. "I didn't even know where that was. So I pick it up, I'm like, 'Hello?' and someone says, 'Hello. This is Hugh Hefner.' I was like, 'Fuck you. Yeah, right.' And I hung up." But that was not the end. Hef called her right back and convinced her of his identity and asked her if she'd like to be one of his girlfriends.

"Right there. In my towel," she says, laughing. "I'm like, 'What? I don't believe it.' And he said, 'No, I'm serious, darling. I'm serious.' I'd never even met him!" ※ **BUT THEY DID** meet at the birthday party, and Hef eventually asked her to move in. Kendra took some time making the decision, but kept visiting the Mansion in the meantime. She found that her feelings for Hef were growing, and she took her spot as the final component in the trio that eventually became The Girls Next Door.

You once said on the show that Hef "saved [your] life." Considering all that you had already been through before you met him, what did you mean by that?

When I said he saved my life, I meant that I had just graduated from high school and I didn't know what I wanted to do. I was planning to go to college, but I wasn't really ready for that. I didn't know what I wanted to do. **HEF HELPED GIVE ME DIRECTION.** He helped me motivate myself. He gave me a motivation in life.

What was it like being a Painted Lady?

Being body-painted was really **WEIRD**. I was never really that kind of girl—to be walking around, like, Jack Nicholson all naked. **BUT I HAD A LOT OF FUN.** I had a great time. I met [Eagles quarterback] Donovan McNabb that night! I met Donovan McNabb when I was naked. And I first met Hef naked. It was just weird meeting all these celebs while I was naked. It was cool and I had a lot of fun, but it was weird.

What are some of the hard parts about living your life on TV?

I have the worst case of acne that you could ever see. Seriously. I've been on Accutane for almost five months now. And I'm doing the show at the same time. So I've got cameras in my face when I don't really want them there. And now my acne's in, like, HD! It's really embarrassing, but I have to live through it.

Considering you are such an expert in ass-shaking, do you have any tips to share?

I *do* have a secret. **I HAVE A NICE ASS AND EVERYTHING,** but it's not big. It's just a normal ass. But here's the thing: it's all in what you wear. You don't even have to have an ass. It's not even your ass. If you wear pants that are too tight, you can't move. You have to wear a skirt that's a little poofy. Not really tight or anything. That's what you want to wear when you're booty-shaking, because you see more things shaking. Just like a hula.

What do you think when people, especially young girls, say they want to be just like you?

I don't really like it. I never looked up to anybody. I did what I did. When I fell, I picked myself back up. I didn't have anybody picking me up. I never looked at someone's life and thought, "Aw, man, I want to be just like her. Maybe if I do the things she does I can be like that." That wasn't me. I did what I wanted to do, what my heart told me. That's why in the celebrity rap superstar show I did, I wrote a rap that went, *"Little girl be you, cause I gotta be me./Live your own life, be all you can be./And if the sky turns gray, it's okay./Just keep working hard, you'll shine one day."* That goes out to girls who say they want to be me. Because I really hate it when girls say that to me. I'm like, "Be you."

Slam Book of Kendra Wilkinson

As a child, what did you want to be when you grew up?

I really wanted to be a marine biologist. That was one thing I really loved, because growing up in San Diego I was all about the ocean and being by the water and the aquarium.

Today, what do you want to be when you grow up?

I'm an entrepreneur. I have so many different things I want to be. I can't make up my mind. So I'm just going to do everything!

What are your turn-ons and turnoffs?

My turn-ons are athletic people and people who have a sense of humor. My turnoffs are mean people and pretty boys.

Who was the first boy you kissed?

I think I had sex with the first boy I kissed. So the first guy I had sex with was the first kiss I had.

What was your best Halloween costume as a child?

I came to school one day for Halloween and I stuffed my boobs with tissue and walked around like I was Jenny McCarthy.

What was the name of your childhood pet?

I had a couple different cats. They died and we got new ones. Buddy, Diablo, Misty, Fluffy, and Kitty. Kitty was my favorite cat. When she died it was the saddest day of my life.

What's your sign? Gemini.

What is your favorite . . .

Food? Philly cheesesteaks. **Color?** Blue. **Number?** Twenty-one.

Movie? The Godfather movies. Our Song. I like movies that are real, that are based on struggling teens, because I grew up sort of like that.

Movie that Hef introduced you to? Somewhere in Time.

Disney character? Belle. **TV show?** The Sopranos.

Book? I like books that help me, like "How to be a better you" and stuff like that. I think my favorite books are probably Go Ask Alice and A Child Called "It" because those books meant something to me. Those books are very intense.

Singer/Band? Growing up I worshipped Janet Jackson, all the West Coast hip-hop: Tupac and N.W.A, and Wu-Tang Clan. I'd say Wu-Tang's my favorite.

Sport (to play)? At the moment, I'm going to have to say it's a toss-up between golf and softball.

Sport (to watch)? Football.   *Playmate?* Lisa Dergan, July 1998.

A Day in the Life of

Kendra Wilkinson

6:00 If I have something to do, I wake up at six A.M. But if I don't . . .

12:00 I wake up at twelve o'clock on the dot every afternoon. I wake up to *SportsCenter*, see what's going on. See if there's any news. If there's nothing that exciting on *SportsCenter*, then I flip down to *Headline News* to see what's on the news. Then, if nothing's on the news, I flip to XM radio on the TV. They have the best music on there. So I get ready to the music on there. I get ready when the music's on. Take a shower, brush my teeth, masturbate. I order breakfast. I order the same thing every single day: Cap'n Crunch, soy milk, coffee, and a bowl of oranges, bananas, and apples.

12:45 Leave my room and get some stuff done.

2:00 If it's a beautiful day, I go outside and do my workout outside. I go hiking almost every day.

3:00 Whatever comes up workwise. Stuff for the show. PR. Check in on my real estate. Business opportunities. Whatever.

6:00 I might go to the gym to catch my spin class or my ab class.

7:30 Sometimes we go out to dinner.

10:00 If we don't go out, I'll order dinner around ten. I usually have a salad with eggs, cheese, and tomatoes. Then I have a side of grilled lemon chicken. And maybe chicken Rice-A-Roni.

11:00 Watch a movie.

3–3:30 Go to bed. I like to catch a little bit of *Mike & Mike in the Morning* on ESPN2. It's my favorite radio show.

Welcome to the Neighborhood

Executive producer Kevin Burns shares a revealing story of the time he and co-executive producer Scott Hartford took the Girls out to eat early in the show's run. "We took the girls to lunch at the Ivy in Beverly Hills. It was just a little thank-you to celebrate the good ratings and the successful premiere of the first episode and to talk about the rest of the episodes for the first season, because it was likely that E! was going to expand on the initial order of eight episodes we had filmed.

🐰 "WHEN WE CAME out from lunch, there was a group of about five or six photographers outside—as there always are around the Ivy—and they said, 'Oh, there's The Girls Next Door. Can we get your picture?' I think one person said, 'There's Holly,' or 'There's Bridget.' The Girls confided in Scott and me that this was the first time anyone had ever asked to take their picture without Hef. It was the first time they ever felt like anybody cared about who they were without Hef in the picture, let alone knew their names. We were very charmed by that." 🐰 HOW THE GIRLS went from the anonymity of a group of several girlfriends to celebrities in their own right is the story of their lives going from reality to reality TV. In many ways, it was simply a matter of the right pieces falling into place. But this story evolved over years, not months, and included diverse characters like Betty Grable, the Gottis, *Alice in Wonderland*, and a little bit of Arts & Entertainment. 🐰 KEVIN BURNS, a film and television producer based at Twentieth Century Fox Studios, met Hugh Hefner through a mutual friend in the fall of 1994. At the time, Kevin was working on what was to become the acclaimed *Biography* series for the A&E cable network. The first episode he was developing was based on the actress Betty Grable. During one of the nights he was invited to the Mansion, Kevin mentioned the project to Hef, who was on record as having an interest in the classic actress. "Hef starts pouring out his heart to me about how Betty Grable was the woman he designed the original girl next door after," Kevin explains. The conversation helped to cement their friendship. 🐰 AFTER THE FIRST OF HIS *BIOGRAPHY* EPISODES AIRED, Kevin got a call from *Playboy*'s head of publicity telling him that Mr. Hefner was impressed by his work and would like him to produce Hef's *Biography* episode. Kevin was extremely flattered and petitioned A&E to do the show. The response was positive, but they hit a snag right out of the gate. As Kevin explains, "I called Hef up and I said, 'Thank you for recommending me. I'm going to be doing your *Biography*.' And he said, 'How long is the show?' and I said, 'It's an hour.' He asked, 'What kind of an hour? Sixty minutes?' and I said, 'Well, it's about forty-five minutes.'" 🐰 HEF'S RESPONSE? "Oh, that won't do." 🐰 MR. HEFNER DID not feel that his story could be told in a mere forty-five minutes. And when the executives at A&E learned that their subject was offering to open up his vaults and give Kevin access to *everything*, they could not refuse. Thus, Hugh Hefner's episode became the first two-hour *Biography*, and premiered to stellar ratings. Following the success of his first outing with Hef, Kevin continued his relationship with *Playboy*, producing another pair of specials: *Inside the Playboy Mansion*—a tour of the famed estate's history based on the book of the same name—and *Playboy's 50th Anniversary Celebration*, a variety show in the mode of the old *Playboy After Dark* series hosted by Hef in the sixties. 🐰 THINKING HIS TRILOGY of Playboy specials was complete, Kevin was surprised when the executives at A&E came to him again with an idea for a reality show—but not as surprised as he was upon hearing their plan. The network was enjoying great success with a reality show called *Growing Up Gotti*, based on the family of John Gotti's daughter. A&E was interested in building on that success with a new show called *Growing Up Hefner*. Kevin, who admits he was not a fan of the reality-show genre at the time, recalls the pitch: "They wanted to do Hef helping his two sons with their homework and having this kind of across-the-fence relationship with his wife, Kimberley. It would be kind of *Upstairs, Downstairs*, with the butlers rolling their eyes at the outrageous requests made by Hefner and the Girls while Mrs. Hefner is next door trying to make sure the kids get a good education in this world of hedonism." Kevin cringed at the idea, but agreed to take it to Mr. Hefner. **HEF'S RESPONSE?** "These people don't have a clue who I am." **CONSIDERING A&E HAD** been so good to the pair with all of their specials, Kevin and Hef worked with the network to come up with a new idea. Hef was insistent that anything they did had to meet three criteria: first was that he would do it only with Kevin, which the producer considered a tremendous honor; the second was that Hef didn't want to do a cruel show, like so many of the other reality shows on television—he insisted that no one's feelings could be hurt; and finally, he agreed to do it only if it was fun, because there was no way A&E could pay him the money to do it otherwise. **"I HAD BEEN ASKED** to do variations on the theme a number of times before," Hef says. "I felt it would be an intrusion. Other reality shows were so contrived, so downscale. It didn't really make a lot of sense to me." But Hef reiterates that his trust in Kevin Burns was the key to making this new show a reality. "The Girls themselves had mixed emotions about it. Holly particularly had reservations. She was afraid—with understandable reason—that it might screw up an otherwise ideal relationship. But we decided to go ahead and do it.

And, of course, we were totally unprepared for what it turned out to be."  **KEVIN ASSEM-BLED** a team to film a couple days at the Mansion and put together a brief presentation for the network. "We thought we were going to do about eight minutes," he recalls. "It turned out to be twenty-two. It was a pilot we called *Hef's World*. And we still thought it was going to be *Upstairs, Downstairs*. We thought it was going to be Hef and his girlfriends and his friends living their fun lifestyle, with the staff occasionally commenting on the madcap high jinks." The events surrounding Bridget's upcoming birthday were chosen as the jumping-off point for the episode and they got to work, squeezing everything into two days of filming. **A&E LOVED IT.** But at the time they were dealing with concerns that the network was moving too far from the "Arts" side of their name. So, in spite of their appreciation of the show they had inspired, they had to take a pass. But the idea was not dead. While Kevin and his business partner, Scott Hartford, were meeting with friends at the E! network, they brought up their pilot. There was interest and a request to see the tape, which was still being discussed under the *Hef's World* concept. Once the tape was sent, the response was immediate. Within a day, Kevin had received a call from his friends at E!, who not only loved the idea but *got* the idea. "[Senior VP of Programming Development] Lisa Berger looked at this pilot and said, 'I want to know those girls. I want to see this world through their eyes. This is *Alice in Wonderland*. And I want to see Wonderland through Alice.'" The production went back for another day to film interviews with the Girls, which had not been done for the original presentation. With those interviews in place, the network was sold on the series and greenlit eight episodes in May of 2005, to air in August of 2005. **FROM THERE IT** was a mad dash to develop the series, though many people involved were still skeptical it would even last a full season. "Maybe some men will tune in for the voyeuristic entertainment, but it probably won't last," people said. "It'll go three episodes and burn out." The skepticism was immediately proven wrong when the series premiered to huge ratings. "Each season it has become more popular than before," Hef proudly notes. "There was always a fascination and curiosity about life at the Playboy Mansion. With *The Girls Next Door* that turned into something more. It not only personalized my life, but also the lives of the Girls. The interconnection of the Girls became hugely fascinating to women—women of all ages, but young women in particular. The sub line on the DVD says it well: 'We call it a fantasy. They call it home.'" **THEY CLEARLY HAD** a hit, and the initial order of eight episodes was bumped up to fourteen. Most agree that the success is due, in large part, to Hef and the Girls, but also stems from the fact that the show is not about the negative catfighting often seen on reality TV. The "wish fulfillment" aspect of *The Girls Next Door* is about the interesting lives these people lead and the exciting things they get to do. This was vital to the Girls as they entered into a series about their unique relationship with Hef. "It's very important to me that it gets reflected the proper way," Bridget says, "that people have a proper

understanding of it, because people do automatically think, 'Oh, it's sleazy' or 'They're sluts' or whatever. And it's not like that. There's a definite relationship here, and a love, but it's also very family-like. We enjoy one another's company. We enjoy just sitting around watching TV and playing games together. I'm happy that the show reflects us that way." ❧ **ONE SEASON LED** to another, and then another. Now the Girls are actively involved in the show's production, making sure that it not only reflects their lives but continues to be new and different every season. Before filming starts on a new season, the producers get together with the Girls to go over their calendars and make sure the cameras catch the most interesting events in the coming months. "The first year, it was just kind of our day-to-day lives and the annual events that go on at the Mansion," Holly explains. "Because every year we have a routine and we celebrate certain holidays and certain events. After a couple of seasons of that they wanted to expand a little bit and follow us traveling, so the show wouldn't become like *Groundhog Day*, showing us doing the same exact thing every year. We're lucky because the show has provided us with a lot of opportunities for growth. The three of us are moving in different directions. That keeps providing the show with new material." ❧ **THEY MAY BE** moving in different directions with those new opportunities, but Kendra recognizes that the show has given back to them personally as well. "Doing the show kind of brought us together," she notes. "I didn't really like it at first, and I had really strict boundary issues with the production. But the more we did it, the more I started liking it. I still hate watching myself on TV. I hate it with a passion. But it gave me an idea of who I really am. It's weird. Watching myself, I learn about myself on TV." ❧ **AS THESE THREE** Girls—these three *women*—learn about themselves, so does the world, and so do the people around them. Kevin Burns continues to be amazed by Holly, Bridget, and Kendra, and he shares the story of the time he and Scott re-created their initial celebratory lunch and brought the Girls back to the Ivy for dinner to commemorate the pickup of their fifth season. "Scott and I had this very nice dinner with the three of them to talk about their ideas for the upcoming season," Kevin recalls. "When we left the restaurant, they were mobbed. I mean *mobbed*. And it was scary. Like *piranhas*. 'Bridget! Kendra! Over here! Holly!' TMZ. Everybody." ❧ **"WITH GIANT POSTERS** for them to sign," Scott adds. ❧ **"PROPS. MEMORABILIA. CALENDARS.** Issues of the magazine," Kevin continues. "The Girls were charming. Smiling. We were like, 'Do you want to go back inside? Do you want us to get some security?' They said, 'No, we're okay. We're okay.' And they signed for everybody. There were children there. There were old people there. But what strikes me is that nothing prepares anybody for being on television. Nothing prepares anyone for stardom. These women, with their own natural instinct, have handled themselves in the press, in the public eye, so much better than I think anybody could expect. It's such a compliment to Hef, and to *Playboy*."

Season 1

⊰ Meet the Girls ⊱

Holly, Bridget, and Kendra show us around the Mansion before preparing for a glamorous night on the town with Hef . . . and a few other girls. The event is a star-studded **American Film Institute** tribute for famed producer/director **George Lucas**. *Star Wars* fan Holly gets into the spirit of the festivities by putting her hair in a Princess Leia do.

Holly: At the end of the episode they show Kendra coming in to get a movie and they make it look like I'm really jealous and really pissed that she came in. Then they cut to me in an interview saying, "I think Hef needs to get rid of the other girls." But when I said that, they were asking me about my whole journey with Hef and about the original seven girlfriends. And I told them, "You know, that situation wasn't working. I think Hef needs to get rid of those other girls." So they put that quote in there to kind of dramatize it a little bit, but [she shrugs it off] whatever.

The luncheon to announce Tiffany Fallon as Playmate of the Year is held at the Mansion, and the Girls host some potential Playmates who have come out to test for the magazine. With all these Playmates around, Bridget laments the fact that she has never been chosen to do a spread in the magazine . . . until Hef announces that the trio will have their own pictorial, and maybe a cover.

Bridget: Being in Playboy *was the number one thing for me from a very young age. As soon as I saw those pages, I knew that was what I wanted to be. I didn't see it for the nudity, I saw it for, "Ah, these girls are beautiful. I hope I'm beautiful like that when I grow up." Then every guy in high school was talking about* Playboy. *I had friends who had the Centerfolds hanging on their walls. It became my standard of beauty.*

Happy Birthday, Kendra!

Hef takes the Girls to the Playboy Jazz Festival at the Hollywood Bowl, which is a considerable undertaking for the staff, requiring them to use the "big bus," a mobile home with all the comforts of home. It's a great way to open Kendra's birthday weekend. The celebration continues when Holly and Bridget go last-minute shopping for party supplies for a luau in the birthday girl's honor and Kendra's family comes up from San Diego for a visit.

Kendra: *You can have big birthdays with a bunch of people there. You can go traveling to Vegas and be around crazy people acting wild. But there's nothing like being with a small group of people who really care about you on your birthday. There's nothing like it.*

What Happens in Vegas

A trip to Sin City to celebrate the birthday of 2004's Playmate of the Year, Carmella DeCesare, gets off to a slow start when Kendra can't find her present. It's only a quick trip out of town for the Girls, who have to be back at the Mansion for nine o'clock curfew . . . until their plane comes in late.

Bridget: *The producers like to create drama with the editing, implying that Holly and I get irritated with Kendra. And it isn't that we don't ever get bothered by her being late or whatever. But they like to show us rolling our eyes. I specifically will not give them that kind of content. So I know when they're showing me rolling my eyes at Kendra that they took it from somewhere else. We all agreed ahead of time, before we even saw a rough cut of the show, to accept that things are edited a certain way. Not that we don't ever get offended by something on the show, but we try to separate real life from the editing. It's not a drama-based show, but there's a little bit here and there.*

Fight Night

It's Fight Night at the Mansion and among the eight hundred guests is Barbi Benton, Hef's ex-girlfriend from the seventies, which causes some stress for Holly. But Kendra enjoys the event, which is packed with sports stars—and one particularly hunky mannequin. Meanwhile, Bridget adds a new member to the family when she gets a puppy she names Wednesday.

Kendra: *That was my favorite episode of all time. It just showed, really, me. It showed who I really am. You could see my craziness and my sparkle and me having real fun in that episode. Like getting all excited and screaming, "Oh, my God! Peyton Manning!" I don't care what people think about how I act. And the mannequin part was probably my favorite scene of all time. That was real, I'm telling you right now. That was me.*

Operation Playmate

The Girls celebrate the Fourth of July with a massive waterslide down the hill on the Mansion's property. And they get in the patriotic spirit by baking cookies to send in care packages for the troops as part of Operation Playmate. Bridget takes her care package in person to her brother, who is serving at Fort Bragg.

Bridget: I went to North Carolina and spent a few days with my brother when I took him the care package. On my way back from North Carolina, we had a three-hour layover in Atlanta. That was when the lady met us at the airport to give me Wednesday [as seen in "Fight Night"], which is why I was so freaked out about the time in that episode—because we had a connecting flight to make.

Just Shoot Me

It's time for the photo shoot for the Girls' first *Playboy* pictorial. Though nerves affect each of the Girls as they pose for individual shots, they grow much more comfortable as the first day goes on. Day two brings setups for the Girls together, but that takes a stressful turn when the shoot runs long and Bridget has to leave for a final exam while Holly and Kendra finish a great setup in the bathhouse shower. But everything is all right when the crew comes back for a reshoot including all three Girls.

Holly: I knew what the magazine was when I was really young because my dad had a subscription. When my parents would get the subscription in the mail, they would look for the Rabbit on the cover. So I immediately thought it was a game. I thought, "This is something interesting!" But they were like, "No, no. This isn't for kids." And then one day when my parents were out of the house, my sister and I found the magazines. We just thought it was hilarious, because there's a naked ass in a magazine. It was the funniest thing we had ever seen.

Midsummer Night's Dream

While the staff prepares the Mansion for the Midsummer Night's Dream party, the Girls help Bridget's sister, Anastasia, get ready with a total makeover, glamming her up *Playboy* style. They go shopping for the perfect outfit and hit the spa, where she gets waxed. In related news, Gizmo goes to the groomer.

Kendra on the Midsummer Night's Dream party: I just love the colors and the whole way it's decorated. It's like everybody comes to that party because it's the biggest one of the year. The best thing about it is, everybody has a Halloween party. Everybody has a New Year's party. Everybody's jumping around to different parties those times of year. But nobody has a Midsummer party. And that's when everybody comes to the Mansion. It's one big, huge party.

TRIPLE PLATINUM PICTORIAL

PLAYBOY

.com • NOVEMBER 2005

AFTER THE PARTY
WITH
JAMIE
FOXX
A BRASH
PLAYBOY
INTERVIEW

20Q
STEVE CARELL

PLUS:
WINTER COATS, HARVEY PEKAR, AN NFL TRAGEDY

WITH
THE
IN BED
GIRLS
NEXT DOOR
E!'S HOT NEW SHOW

SPECIAL
PHOTO FEATURE
DANCING WITH THE STARS'
KELLY
MONACO

Under the Covers

Things aren't always black and white for the Girls when they shoot their *Playboy* cover not knowing if it will actually run on the magazine. While they wait to learn the news, Holly makes over the Mansion guesthouse and throws a barbecue at the Playmate house across the street for the Playmates staying there. The Girls finally learn their fate when the magazine is released—featuring their very first *Playboy* cover.

Holly: Way back when I was in high school, I read Jenny McCarthy's book, and she talked about coming to the Mansion for the first time and staying in the Playmate guesthouse. And I had a vision of what it should look like. I thought it would have different themed rooms and that everything would be all done up with Playboy stuff and really cute. Then I came here and it was really run-down and musty, and done in this old country style. Nothing about it was what I'd imagined. Since I had to redecorate it without spending a lot of money, I had to keep a little bit of the country style. So I went with a shabby-chic look, and I think it's really cute now.

Ghostbusted

Bridget's favorite holiday, Halloween, is celebrated with another blowout and a haunted house. In keeping with the spooky theme, Bridget arranges for a paranormal investigator to explore the Mansion and a medium to host a séance. She hopes to contact the ghost that haunts the place, rumored to be the wife of the original owner. When neither exercise gives them the answers they are looking for, Hef shows the Girls the horror movie he made while in high school to help raise their spirits.

Bridget: I believe the Mansion is haunted, but not by any negative ghost. I think it's a positive thing. I think it's people who have been here in the past. I don't think it's Mrs. Letts at all. I don't even think that Mrs. Letts died in this house, contrary to the ghost story. There's nothing to support that in the research I've done, although it's not one hundred percent clear. If anything it could be Mr. Letts. But I think it's really more recent ghosts and things of Playboy's past.

Grape Expectations

Road trip! It's a loooong day out for the Girls when Bridget takes them on a tour of her hometown of Lodi in Northern California. They go grape-stomping and visit her grandma's house (and see the creepy doll that traumatized Bridget in her childhood) before ending their day at a cigar bar, where it seems half the population has come out to see the hometown girl and her friends.

Bridget: This was one of the first episodes we did. I feel like I could do it differently and better if we went now and spent more time with it. We had to drive the six hours there at the crack of dawn, hurry up and do everything, and drive all the way back that night. We got to spend a lot more time in everyone else's hometown, so I wish I could have done it differently. But it was before Hef was really excited about letting us spend a lot of time out. We still had fun, though. It was still great to have everyone see my grandma's house, because I feel like that's home to me.

I'll Take Manhattan

The Girls travel to New York City with Hef to promote their issue of *Playboy*. They see the sights and meet the fans in a whirlwind tour of the Big Apple. All is not happy travels, though, when they have to deal with an itinerary that includes intensive media coverage and an unpleasant experience on *The View*. But the trip ends on a high note, with a big party in their honor.

Kendra on visiting with the ladies of The View: We're better than them in our hearts, and that's all we need to know. We're open and we're free-spirited. We're not conservative, stuck-up women. We love life and we love to live our lives. In the end, that's all that matters.

My Kind of Town

The Playboy publicity tour moves on to Hef's hometown of Chicago, where he takes the Girls to Playboy headquarters, the original Playboy Mansion, and his childhood home. While they're gone, the Mansion maintenance crew uses the time to work on major household projects. Though the Girls enjoy the trip, they are glad to get home to their puppies (and Gizmo).

Holly on visiting the building that was the original Playboy Mansion: That building was just beautiful. It's so much more beautiful in person than in any of the pictures I've ever seen of it. I wish Hef still owned it. We could have turned it into this awesome hotel or something. It would make a cute boutique hotel. It's such a great building.

Clue-*less*

Holly takes Hef's classic car for a ride after deciding this would be the perfect time to learn how to drive a stick shift. The Mansion hosts a charity tennis tournament, in which Kendra is one of the players in a mixed-doubles match with Playmate Destiny Davis and the Jensen brothers. Bridget hosts a murder mystery/scavenger hunt party for her birthday, where the guests dress in costumes from the twenties and thirties and the murderer turns out to be the birthday girl.

Kendra on the editing that implies she's not as good at sports as she really is: That's what they do to me. They make me sound like, "Yeah, I'm such an athlete. I'm so good at this." Then I do one little thing wrong, and they show it over and over, like I did it wrong a million times. I get so mad about it.

It's Vegas, Baby

Hef and the Girls head to Vegas to promote the upcoming opening of the Playboy Club at the Palms. There's a fashion show to reveal the new Bunny costume as designed by Roberto Cavalli and worn by Holly. While in town, the Girls and Hef go on a shopping spree at the Playboy store, visit the wax version of Hef at Madame Tussauds, and, of course, party at the Palms.

Holly: I really like Vegas a lot. It is just a crazy, crazy place where anything can happen. You can be as crazy as you want to be. You can dream as big as you want. It's a lot like L.A. in that you can dream really big and do what you want and people won't dog you for it. It's a place where anything can happen and people don't judge. The sky's the limit there. I really love it.

The Playboy Mansion

PLAYMATE
HOUSE

HUGH HEFNER'S PATH to the famed estate in the Holmby Hills section of Los Angeles began years before the man even knew the property existed. Mr. Hefner established the Playboy empire in his hometown of Chicago in 1953, editing the first issue of the magazine in his small Hyde Park apartment. The success of the magazine allowed him to buy a residence in the noted Gold Coast section of town by the end of the decade. It was christened the Playboy Mansion. **THE PLAYBOY BRAND** became so popular that it spun off from the magazine into the Playboy Clubs and a Chicago-based television show known as *Playboy's Penthouse*. By the mid-sixties a new version of the series, titled *Playboy After Dark*, was developed as a West Coast production. It was on the second episode of that show that Hef met one of his most famous girlfriends—and frequent guest on *The Girls Next Door*—Barbi Benton. **"FROM THAT POINT** on, I began splitting my time between Chicago and Los Angeles," Hef recalls. While in L.A., he lived in a penthouse of a building on Sunset Boulevard that had a club on the first several floors. "Barbi kept making a case for me getting a house out here," he explains. "I didn't figure that I could find anything comparable to what I had in Chicago. The house I had in Chicago was actually seventy rooms. It had no grounds, but inside it was like a hotel. You could get lost in it. It had all the wonderful paraphernalia: the indoor pool, the underwater bar, the rotating bed. All the toys. I didn't think that I could match it." **THAT DIDN'T STOP** Barbi from location-scouting, though she had to do it on the sly. "Allegedly, she was looking for a place where we could play tennis," Hef says. "But she was really looking for a house that would somehow intrigue." Barbi found such a house, and Hef purchased the Playboy Mansion West for $1.05 million. (That's a bargain today, but in 1971 it was the most money ever spent on a private residence in Southern California.) By 1975 Hef stopped splitting his time between the Playboy Mansions East and West and started living full-time in L.A. For a boy who grew up with dreams of Hollywood, it was like coming home. **NOT THAT THE** residence was perfect the way he found it. The Tudor mansion, built in 1926, was in the style that Mr. Hefner admired, but it lacked the accoutrements he had grown used to at the Playboy Mansion in Chicago. Hef worked with architect Ron Dirsmith to make the property a showplace that included a private zoo and aviary, gym, the now famous pool and grotto, and, of course, the tennis court that Barbi had been seeking. **TODAY THE PLAYBOY** Mansion is arguably the most famous private residence in the world. Part home, part office, the Mansion serves the varied needs of Hugh Hefner and his guests. It is now also the home of the Girls Next Door, who have each lent their own personal touches to the estate.

1 **FRONT GATE** Nestled in a tiny street in the Holmby Hills section of Los Angeles, a block off Sunset Boulevard, the front entrance to the Playboy Mansion is a gateway to another world. Beyond these gates lies the setting for some of the most famous parties in town, a zoo with more than a hundred animals, and the home of Hugh Hefner and the Girls Next Door.

2 **HEF AND HOLLY'S ROOM** Designed with dark woods and a huge marble bath, this is the bedroom of the master of the house and Holly's small corner of the world. The bathroom is Holly's favorite part of the room, though she's also partial to the upstairs office, where she was recently given rights to the second desk. "It is so helpful because I have this industrial-size printer where I print layouts for Hef to look at, and it's huuuuge," Holly says. "So the fact that he gave me that space to put it is really great, because otherwise I don't know where it would be."

3 **BRIDGET'S ROOM** This pink palace is *the* place to go for party prep and is the home of Gizmo's famous treehouse. While the décor is totally Bridget's choice, it doesn't necessarily reflect her true personality. She says, "When I came to the Mansion, Hef said, 'You can decorate your room however you want.' I really wanted it to be *Playboy* themed, girlie. And so this was my opportunity to do everything pink and crazy girlie. But I really like black. I'm kind of a little bit rock-and-roll, which you would never know from watching the show."

4 **K-DUB'S CRIB** The place where Raskal and Martini reside, among the clutter of Kendra's sports jerseys, pimp cups, and an unidentified pair of panties that continue to resurface no matter how many times she gets rid of them. "My favorite part about my bedroom is my bathtub," says Kendra. "It's a Jacuzzi tub, and I just lie in there for hours and fall asleep. I also like the view from my window. Especially when it rains. It's a beautiful view."

5 **MANSION OFFICES** In this wing you'll find Mary and Norma, as well as the many other members of the Playboy staff who keep the Mansion—and Hef and the Girls—running.

6 **PET CEMETERY** The final resting place for the beloved pets of the Mansion. Here lie Little Foot and Archie—rest in peace.

7 **GAME HOUSE** Housing Playboy pinball machines and classic arcade games from the eighties, this is a popular spot to chill. Bridget hosted Wednesday's birthday party on the outside patio and in the private yard.

8 **TENNIS COURT** The location of the annual Monty Hall/Cedars-Sinai Tennis tournament (in which Kendra, Destiny, and the Jensen brothers fought their epic match, seen in the episode "Clue-*less*"). It is also the spot of the multiroom haunted house setup for the Mansion's annual Halloween party.

9 **GUEST HOUSE** Originally decorated by Barbi Benton, this house is the spot where women stay when they come to test for the magazine, which is why it has been nicknamed the Playmate guest house. Holly gave it a low-budget makeover, taking it from classic country to shabby chic, giving each room a fun, *Playboy*-inspired theme. Guests can now stay in the Bunny Room, the Playmate of the Year Room, the Pamela Anderson Room, or the Marilyn Monroe Room.

10 **AVIARY** This spot houses much of the Mansion's bird population, lizards, and exotic flowers and plants, as well as the tropical aquariums that Holly added new residents to for her and Hef's fifth anniversary.

11 **BATH HOUSE/GYM** Fully stocked for visitors of the Mansion, the bath house also boasts the tropical shower where Holly, Bridget, and Kendra filmed part of their first *Playboy* photo shoot. Beneath the bath house is a full-size gym, also recently redesigned and updated by Holly.

12 POOL AND GROTTO Arguably the most famous pool in the world, this is the location of many Sunday Fun in the Sun parties. The infamous grotto houses four separate hot tubs and served as another location in the Girls' first *Playboy* photo shoot.

13 BACKYARD Home to koi ponds and roaming flamingos, peacocks, and cranes, this is the prime party spot at the Mansion. Tented off and decorated for special events, the yard takes on different themes throughout the year, becoming un-recognizable from its typical day-to-day appearance.

14 Conceived under a "minimum-confinement" philosophy, the Mansion zoo hosts many exotic birds and three primate facilities. The most famous resident, Coco the spider monkey, continues to do well in life, if not on her diet. A colony of squirrel monkeys is another highlight—guests can feed them grapes and bananas kept in a container by their cage.

15 The sloping lawn at the side of the Mansion is now the spot for the custom water-slide that has become the highlight of the annual Fourth of July party.

(OFF PHOTO) PLAYMATE HOUSE A separate residence on a neighboring street, the Playmate House is for longer-term stays for Mansion guests. Women hoping to make Los Angeles a permanent residence might live there while getting acclimated to the city. It is where one can find Hef's famed round bed from the original Playboy Mansion, as well as a replica of the chair he sat in for the iconic photograph of him holding the first issue of *Playboy*.

Mansion Staff

WHEN MEMBERS OF the staff are asked how long they have worked at the Playboy Mansion, the answer is more likely to come in terms of decades than years. Hugh Hefner enjoys a close bond with his employees. "There's a lot of loyalty in this house," says Security Supervisor Joe Piastro. "We are a family. We look after one another. There are times when we're at each other's throats, but that's the nature of the game. We're a big family and we enjoy working here. I know I do. We get the job done and we also have fun doing it, so that makes it quite rewarding." 🐰 **JOE, ALONG WITH** Hank Fawcett in Construction and Maintenance, are among those who have worked at the Mansion almost as long as Hef has owned the property. Hank sums up his work responsibilities simply by saying, "My one job is to please Mr. Hefner. That is my only job here. And that's all I really want to do. When I'm setting up Hef's parties I want to give him something that he can come out and go, 'Wow. I really like that.' Now, with the Girls participating, I want *them* to say that, too. And if they want to participate in the design or give ideas or anything, I welcome it." 🐰 **FEW PEOPLE AT** the Mansion have been with Hef as long as his personal assistant, Mary O'Connor, who has worked with the man since 1969 (give or take a few years; she left on two occasions, but kept coming back). "I spend more time with Hef than I do with any other person in my life," Mary admits of their long-standing relationship. "Even though he may be in one room and I'm in another room—because I'm never right in his face. I'm never right in his presence. That's my choice, and what I feel my role is. But I know everything that's going on. I kind of see myself as a voyeur." 🐰 **THOUGH SHE WOULD** be loath to hear it, some consider Mary to be the breakout star of *The Girls Next Door*. The no-nonsense, straight-talking, motherly figure is more likely to converse about sex than about baking cookies. Her boyfriend of more than two decades, Captain Bob, is a de facto member of the Playboy family as well, enjoying *Monday Night Football* with Kendra and even building the cake that Bridget popped out of on Hef's eightieth birthday. The extended family reaches out

Mary O'Connor

Brian Olea

to relatives of many of the staff. Not that most of them ever imagined they would be able to say that. ❦ "I THINK A lot of people never planned on this being their permanent gig," says Brian Olea from Guest Services. "It was supposed to be one of those sideline gigs: 'This will be fun to do while we work on something else, focusing on our careers.' It's amazing how this place captures you. All of a sudden you're part of this family, and that's very hard to leave because of the relationships we have with the staff and the family." ❦ THOUGH THEIR JOBS may be varied, there is one thing they have in common when it comes to working at the Playboy Mansion: like the old credit card slogan, membership does have its privileges. "It's an interesting place to work," notes Norma Maister. "It opens a lot of doors. Just by me being a woman and calling somewhere, I can get anything done. All I say is, 'Hi, it's Norma from the Playboy Mansion,' and I know what they're thinking. Especially if it's a guy. They don't picture the Agnes Gooch of me; they picture one of these lovely Girls. Believe me, I take real advantage of it." These days, though, with the success of the show, the people on the other end of the line are just as likely to be a little starstruck, knowing exactly who they are talking to.

A Few Words from the Mansion Staff . . .

. . . ON BEING PART OF THE SHOW

CARLENA BRYANT: We were always trained to get away from the cameras. Like when Hef's being photographed, you don't want to be in the background. So it was hard in the beginning to actually realize, "Oh, I'm supposed to be here. Oh, okay." And it's still taken me a while to get used to. For instance, how I really am with Kendra off-camera is different than what you see. It's more comfortable off-camera, because I always think a lot about what I say to her when we're being filmed. It's kind of awkward.

JON DAVIS (J.D.): Now I don't even see the cameras. At first it made me a little nervous, but it actually didn't take that long to adjust. They were just scenery after a while. They'll ask me if I want to do something for a particular scene, and I'm like, "Sure." You get kind of nervous when they're first putting the mike on you. You're like, "Oh, my goodness." But it's not a big deal anymore.

ALAN LOEB: Every Friday morning when Bridget has her radio show, she calls up at 10:02, and J.D. and I take turns answering the phone. One Friday he does it, one Friday I do it. We have a little dialogue with her. One day they came in and said, "You know, we didn't get your part of the dialogue. Can we do it now?" And

we did it up about a week later. When they put it on the show, I'm thinking, "This isn't anything." But when it actually came on, it worked. So many times I'll be in the pantry doing nothing and then I'll see what I was doing on the show and it fits the story.

BOB COLIN: I tend to shy away from the cameras. I don't really like seeing myself on the camera, but I have a little boy who's eight years old, and he loves the Girls. So he sees the show and he loves it when I'm on there. He looks for me in the background. So if I'm in the background, I'm fine. I'm not in front of the camera, like Norma or Hank or Brian. But if I'm in the background, that's enough for him to say, "There you are, Dad!"

Bob Colin

NORMA MAISTER: I will knock people over to get in front of the camera. There's no question in my mind. The first time they came with the camera, I was very shy. First of all, I'm not a shy person, but I was very shy and I felt very intimidated. But after ten minutes, my mind was going, "I should have been an actress. This is the greatest thing ever!"

. . . ON BEING RECOGNIZED BY THE FANS

BRIAN OLEA: I'll admit that it's weird. I spent all my life trying to pursue music and do that kind of a thing, and I kind of wanted that recognition. Then, leaving that world and coming here, I got used to working in the background. Now, because of the show, I'm in the forefront—well, I'm still in the background, but still somehow seen. It's weird. Because it's not like this character that's made up. It's not like I'm portraying a character. That's me. So I'm like, "Wait a minute, people know me." When people call my name—"Hey, Brian!"—I'm looking around, like, "What?"

MARY O'CONNOR: I had a little girl chase me around Wal-Mart in Branson, Missouri. I'm shopping in Wal-Mart with the ugliest clothes on you could ever imagine. The coat I had on had a hood. It was colder than Billy Hell. And she was chasing me, and she said, "I know who you are. I know you're Mary from *The Girls Next Door*. I love that show!" We also had a guy coming to work on our backyard last summer. I was sitting out on the patio and he finally said, "Excuse me, but I know who you are." So that's fun. But it's very embarrassing for me because I'm not an in-front-of-the-thing person. All I can do is just tell them, "Thank you for watching."

NORMA MAISTER: I was having dinner with my mom and a girlfriend and her mom. This little girl came over—she looked about eleven years old—and stood at the end of the table. We all looked at her, and I thought, "Oh, I know why she's here." It was hysterical because my mother was so proud of me. You would think she was sitting with Bette Davis. It was, "Oh, yes, this is my daughter!" and "Oh, yes, she's on TV!" And truthfully, I like it.

ALAN LOEB: I was coming out of the theater and I was waiting for my wife and just standing there and a young girl, thirteen or fourteen years old, came running up to me. She said, "I saw you in Kendra's bedroom! I know you've been in Kendra's bedroom!"

JON DAVIS (J.D.): I've actually gotten some contacts from as far back as high school. I get people who see me. My nieces and nephews are like, "Hey, that's my uncle!" It's very interesting. One night I was at a restaurant and somebody recognized me. I got fifty percent off my meal. I was like, "Hey, I'll work it that way till I can't."

Top:
Norma Maister

Above:
Alan Loeb

. . . ON THE GIRLS

MARY O'CONNOR: This is the best. Absolutely the best. Because these are really nice girls, and they have aspirations of being better people and motivating themselves. They're not demanding. They're just great girls, really great girls.

Holly is probably the first of Hef's girlfriends that I feel like she's a daughter to me. I feel like we talk about things in her life and we share more than any of the other girls who have ever been around. Holly has an agenda, like everybody else. But her agenda is Hef. It's not what she can get. It's not that she's only going to be here for a year. Her agenda is totally Hef. And so she's very good. She's just a good person. Very smart. Very articulate.

NORMA MAISTER: I've watched the Girls from the time they came to now. They've grown up. They're much more sophisticated than they were when they first came. They're much more worldly because they've traveled and they've just absorbed it all. I think it's just great that they're getting an education as well as doing the show. It's really nice. They're very nice girls. There's a genuine warmth between us all. They care about us and we care about them, but not to the point where it's gooey.

They always remember me, which I find very sweet. Bridget always brings me Hanukkah cookies, which I like. They're tiny little dreidels and things, and they're adorable. This year she brought me a case because last year she bought me a box and I said, "Oh, my family loved these. Where did you get them?" So she bought me a case.

Kendra's just very lovely and very generous. She's very warm. You can tease her about anything. She's a riot. She's an absolute riot.

JON DAVIS (J.D.): Holly is the quiet, reserved one. The good thing about the show is I get to see Holly in a different light. She keeps to herself, but she's very approachable, too. That goes for all three of the Girls. All three of them are very approachable and very easygoing.

One thing I like about Bridget, in my experience with her, is that she always has a smile on her face. No matter how busy or crazy it is, she's always like, "Hey, J.D.!" She always takes that moment.

Kendra is just funny. Kendra's from San Diego, and I was born and raised in Los Angeles and she's a sports nut, so we have that little battle. She loves the Padres. I love the Dodgers. So we love to rib each other in that regard. She's just very easy and natural.

JOE PIASTRO: I've been on escorts with the Girls where fans wanted their autographs. I've seen the Girls autograph cell phones, shoes, breasts, arms, elbows—you name it. It's crazy. They understand that they wouldn't be in that position if it wasn't for the fans. They understand that. It's like when we go to the airport—whether we're leaving or arriving—they're recognized. And they're gracious.

. . . ON BEING IN THE SHOW'S OPENING ANIMATION

HANK FAWCETT: It was cool. The first thing we wanted was our own bobble-heads. But what about that cheap-ass Kevin [Burns]! He didn't give us any of those little bobble-heads. What's the deal with that?

CARLENA BRYANT: They just stopped me one day and said, "Can we get a photo of you for, possibly, the show?" I'm like, "Okay." Then I was off for two days and I got back on Friday and everybody was like, "You're a bobble-head." I'm like, "What? How are you going to call me that? I'm kind of smart!" They said, "No, you're a bobble-head in the opening." I said, "Okay?" It took me seeing it to understand what they were talking about. But—typical girl—I was like, "Oh, I wish I would have known, I would have done my hair better."

BRIAN OLEA: I was quite excited about that. "Yeah! I'm a bobble-head!" I remember they took me out back and said, "Brian, we've got a surprise. We're not telling you what it is. Do you mind? We've got to take some snapshots." I'm like, "Yeah, okay, whatever." Any request, you say yes and you do it. And then when it came out they were like, "That's what we were doing!" And I was like, "I'm a bobble-head! All right. So when do we get 'em?" I want my bobble-head. I have people who are dying for my bobble-head, just so they can smack it around.

From top: J.D. Davis, Joe Piastro, Hank Fawcett

Calendar of Events

(Mansion events and dates are always subject to change)

February: Mardi Gras party
(usually the weekend after Valentine's Day)

March: Playboy Golf Scramble

April 9: Hef's Birthday and annual party weekend,
with Casablanca Night

May–September: Fun in the Sun Sundays

June 12: Kendra's Birthday

June: Playboy Jazz Festival
(Father's Day weekend)

July: Fourth of July party

August: Midsummer Night's Dream party (first weekend of the month)

September: Monty Hall/Cedars-Sinai Tennis Tournament
(toward end of month)

September 25: Bridget's Birthday

October: Halloween party (the weekend before Halloween)

December 23: Holly's Birthday

December 31: New Year's Eve party

The Mansion Parties

New Year's Eve

HEF: New Year's Eve is a combination of black-tie and lingerie. Because people go from one party to another on New Year's Eve, we keep it so that people can come in formal wear or pajamas. There's also something delicious about the notion of guys in formal attire and girls in lingerie. Naughty and nice.

HOLLY: The New Year's Eve party is different from the other parties. It's smaller, first of all. People don't stay as long, because they party-hop all over town, and it doesn't really last very long. Everyone kind of splits right after midnight.

BRIDGET: For New Year's Eve Hef always does a black-tie evening with a black-and-white checkerboard dance floor and traditional decorations. This past year, I convinced him to switch it up and do it as Winter Wonderland, with a white carpet, a solid white dance floor that looked almost like an ice-skating rink, little white twinkle lights, and white birch trees lining the room. It was beautiful.

KENDRA: My favorite part of the New Year's Eve party is the kiss.

ALAN LOEB: I'm one of Mr. Hefner's party butlers. I stay with him the whole night, getting whatever he needs. I'm there for almost every party. When they asked me to work New Year's Eve, I told them I actually spend that night with my wife. We go out to dinner. So my boss, Brian, said to me, "Ask your wife if she wants to come and work. She doesn't have to do anything. It's just to have her here. Then at midnight you two can be together and celebrate New Year's." Well, I didn't think my wife would go for it at all, but when I explained it to her she said, "Wow! That's great!" She's done it for five years now. Every year we come, she works the VIP table, and at a quarter to twelve or so she comes in to see me. When all the balloons come down, Bridget will come over and give her a hug and wish her a happy new year. She and Bridget know each other now. That's made it a lot of fun.

BOB COLIN: For the parties, I work at the parking lot where they come in and get on the bus. I'm one of the people who take the Polaroids of the girls for Mr. Hefner's files. I take the pictures and put names on the Polaroids, for what girls might come back for other parties, or maybe for the magazine. He may see someone who catches his eye, and if he looks at the picture he can say, "Okay, let's call this girl."

Fourth of July

HOLLY: My favorite party is definitely Fourth of July. It's different from our other parties because it's a backyard barbecue and it's during the day. We have our awesome waterslide, which was my idea. We have the best barbecue and junk food. It's a long day. The only nighttime part is when it first gets dark and we have fireworks. Hef plays backgammon, and I can just hang out with all my friends, have a few drinks, play volleyball. I just love it.

KENDRA: I love playing volleyball on the Fourth of July, and watching the fireworks, and all the great food. I don't really do the waterslide because the water's cold and for some reason every Fourth of July I'm sick. Every *single* Fourth of July I'm sick. So I'm already freezing. I don't want to go down this cold waterslide.

BRIDGET: There are so many different aspects to the party. It's great that everyone's around for the big barbecue. I love the waterslide. I really love the fireworks. I get emotional during the fireworks. It's just a wonderful day.

HUGH HEFNER: It's everything you would expect for an old-fashioned Fourth of July, with bathing suits and volleyball and waterslides, a New Orleans band, and everything like that. And it's patriotic as hell. It's just an old-fashioned holiday. I like the Fourth of July a lot.

Midsummer Night's Dream

HEF: The parties that are the most popular, I think, are the pajama and lingerie parties. The notion of a Playboy pajama party is immediately very attractive and appealing to people. I think the most popular of those is the Midsummer Night's Dream party. It is a pajama and lingerie party with Painted Ladies, and it's done with a very romantic Midsummer Night's Dream theme. Last year we did it with a little bit of an Arabian connection. But the parties are essentially still the same.

HOLLY: That's the biggest party, along with Halloween. It's a big extravaganza. It's a lot of fun. People are encouraged to dress up. You don't know what to expect.

BRIDGET: The decorations are my favorite part, even when we just do the traditional Midsummer Night's Dream theme. It's kind of Shakespearean with all the little white twinkle lights and the flowers. It's such a beautiful party and it really transforms the Mansion. You wouldn't even know you were in the backyard if somebody blindfolded you and just put you in there.

KENDRA: I like the Midsummer Night's Dream party because it's the biggest party of the year. Nobody else has a Midsummer Night's Dream party. It's very enchanting. It looks like you're in the middle of a fantasy place. Like you're trippin' on 'shrooms or something. There are all these bright, vibrant colors. It's just really fun. That's my favorite party.

HANK FAWCETT: I wanted to do something special for the Millennium party. I'm talking to Mr. Hefner about the whole thing and I'm going, "Okay, what I'd really like to do is . . . I think I'd like to do go-go girls onstage. What do you think?" Well, he wasn't *really* hot on that. So I had to go back and think about what the heck I wanted to do. Then I saw some pictures of body painting, and I went, "Well, what if we do nude painting?" He wasn't quite sure about that, but he was open to the idea. It was certainly better than go-go girls. But the funniest thing about it was, there'd be people—and remember, this was the first time we'd done it, and I'd never seen it before anyplace else. These girls were onstage and the light wasn't so bright that you knew exactly what they looked like, but they were very well painted. They were really nicely done. And they were onstage and people were dancing and honest to God, they stopped on

the dance floor and just gawked at these women. It was the craziest thing. Guys, gals, didn't matter. They couldn't believe what they saw. So it became a staple for all our subsequent parties.

NORMA MAISTER: I'm in charge of the Painted Ladies. We have twelve Painted Ladies for Hef's parties. It is my job to make sure that they stick to their schedule. Two of them are on the stage dancing and two of them are passing out Jell-O shooters. And I make sure they are not bothered by anybody, because if they are, they can come to me. It's easier for me to spot security if there's someone making them uncomfortable, which luckily has never happened. It's my job just to make sure that they behave themselves, to be Bunny Mother and make sure that these girls are doing what they're supposed to.

Halloween

HOLLY: Halloween is amazing. I think my favorite part, besides dressing up, is just the fact that there are so many different things to do. There's the haunted house, the haunted forest, fortune-tellers, people wandering around all over the property trying to scare you. All kinds of things are going on.

BRIDGET: Halloween is my favorite holiday, and the Mansion throws one of the world's best Halloween parties. It has everything: an awesomely scary haunted house, a creepy cemetery full of goblins and pneumatic figures, a wicked forest full of crazy psycho killers, fortune-tellers. And everybody goes all out on their costumes! At the Mansion, we celebrate Halloween for almost a full week, with festivities like going to the pumpkin patch and pumpkin-carving parties, and we find occasion to dress up three or four times. It's the best!

KENDRA: I like Halloween because I love the decorations. It's all so freaky-looking. They really go all out. The decorations are the best part, but I also love the haunted house and the scary people hiding all over the Mansion, waiting to jump out at you.

HANK FAWCETT: Halloween is the best party of the year. It is so over-the-top. Midsummer Night's Dream and Hef's birthday and New Year's are all pretty much in the backyard. That's where the party is, and that's fine, because that's the party. But Halloween, we get to go through the entire Mansion. So now you have this huge addition, if you wish. Halloween is one of those events where anything goes. It doesn't have to be a Frankenstein; it can be a ghoulish monster lying there, bleeding to death. It can be this huge monster that's twenty-five feet tall. With pneumatics. It's all about scaring. I love that aspect. So we take over the front yard. We take over the hillside. We do the tennis court. Everything gets done. And, as I say, anything goes. There are no restrictions on what's allowed.

BRIAN OLEA: Halloween is probably one of my favorites. You have Midsummer Night's Dream and you have Halloween. To me, I like Halloween. I still have the little boy in me who likes to dress up. I think it's fun. It's a time when you can actually become something else. Mr. Hefner allows so much to be done to his property, as far as re-dressing it with the giant graveyard out in the front, and the gargoyles up top. It's just a fun time because the whole place is transformed.

IN DECADES PAST, Mansion residents and friends celebrated Hef's birthday in a variety of wild and wacky ways, from birthday roasts to mock Olympics to something rather interestingly called "the Schlong Show." Today Hef and the Girls are as likely to spend Hef's birthday in Vegas as they are to host another of the Mansion's signature "lingerie or less" parties. Whatever the plan, Hef's birthday weekend is always capped off with his closest friends on Casablanca Night.

The Mansion Party Menu

EXECUTIVE CHEF WILLIAM S. BLOXSOM-CARTER: We want the guests to be surprised to see different types of food coming out throughout the night. Most guests, when they come to Hef's parties, are here for six to eight hours because they're having such a good time with the whole experience. One of the things Mr. Hefner has always emphasized is hospitality and why it's so important to him. It's very rare that you would find, in somebody's home, the level of culinary artistry that we have here, with an executive chef and senior chefs and the whole hierarchy that you would find in a high-end restaurant or hotel. So we really strive to hit all these high marks.

Midsummer Night's Dream Party

PLAYBOY MANSION WEST ✳ AUGUST 4, 2007

The Aladdin's Feast

Jell-O Shooters

Cherry LifeSaver, Grape Hawaiian Punch, and Midori Sour

Crispy Rumaki

Crispy Coconut Shrimp with Mandarin Orange Dip

Curried Risotto Croquettes

Crispy Lamb Wontons with Mint-Lemongrass Dip

Spicy Shrimp Kabobs with Cucumber-Yogurt Dip

Chicken Sausages with Caramelized Onions and Parsley

Charred Beef Brochettes with Honey Mustard–Mint Glaze

Dungeness Crab Cakes with Pineapple-Cilantro Relish

LATE NIGHT CHEF'S OFFERINGS

Roasted Turkey and Cheese Lavosh Wraps

Pita Crisps with Hummus and Baba Ghanoush

Platters of Whole Fresh Fruit

The Sinbad's Feast

SUSHI BAR

Hand-Sliced Tuna and Hamachi, Nigiri, and Maki

Sides of: Soy Sauce, Wasabi, and Pickled Ginger

CHEESE BUFFET

Farmstead Cheeses with Artisan Breads

Candied Pecans, Port-Infused Figs, and Sauterne-Poached Apricots

SEAFOOD DISPLAY

Jumbo Shrimp Cocktail, Crab Claws and Legs, Oysters on the Half Shell

Cocktail Sauce, Ginger-Lemongrass Mignonette Sauce, Lemon Wedges

Midsummer Night's Dream Party

PLAYBOY MANSION WEST ❋ AUGUST 4, 2007

The Sultan's Feast

Pomegranate Glazed Rack of Lamb, Carved Tableside

Lemon Wedges and Pomegranate Gastrique

Glazed Shrimp Brochettes with Garlic Sauce

Coconut Green-Lentil Curry

Chicken Kabobs with Grilled Tomatoes, Onions, and Parsley

Chilled Saffron-Yogurt-Dill Dip

Basmati Rice with Golden Raisins, Lemon, and Parsley

Tabbouleh with Lemon, Diced Tomato, Parsley, and Scallion

Tomato and Cucumber Salad with Heirloom Tomatoes, Red Onions, Kalamata Olives, Feta Cheese,
and Oregano-Lemon–Olive Oil Dressing

Rosemary Grissini, Dates, Feta Cheese, and Seasoned Mediterranean Olives

Wish Granted

Opulently Displayed Petite Dessert Pastries, Macaroons, Chocolate-Dipped Stem Strawberries,
and Hearth-Baked Mansion Cookies

Chocolate River Fondue with Rice Krispies Treats, Marshmallows, Strawberries,
Graham Cracker Dust, Pineapples, and Bananas

*The Buffets Will Be Decorated with Dates, Coconuts, Figs, Banana Leaves, Papayas,
Kiwis, Pineapples, Ginger Flowers, Wild Bananas, and Ferns.*

Party Planning with the Girls Next Door

NOT EVERY PARTY at the Playboy Mansion is a massive blowout with over a thousand guests. The Girls Next Door have hosted a number of smaller soirees for their friends and loved ones, ranging from birthday parties to baby showers to murder mysteries. Here are some of their favorites.

Murder Mystery Party

THESE PARTIES ARE great, especially for large groups. They can be as intricate or as simple as you like. Whether you hire a professional acting troupe to help, buy a premade game, or make it all up on your own, there's an option to fit every budget.

THE GUEST LIST

A Murder Mystery party is an interactive event, so you need to invite people who are outgoing and aren't going to be afraid to get into character. They need to be willing to run around and be an active part of the night. It helps to come up with the characters in advance and create dossiers for each of your guests. The earlier your guests get these, the better prepared they'll be. But throw in some improvisation during the party to keep the guests on their toes. If you have a scavenger-hunt element to the game, let your guests know ahead of time that there may be walking (or running) involved so they can dress appropriately.

PARTY PREPARATIONS

Create the perfect ambiance. Even if you don't live in a Mansion that was built in the twenties, you can use decorations and theme music to help set the mood. This helps to keep people in character and makes the evening fun and exciting. Little touches like hand towels in the restrooms that match the motif of your party will extend the theme even when guests are taking a break.

No matter how careful you are with the guest list, know that it's possible that not all the guests will get into the costume theme. Have a few proper accessories on hand to dress guests who don't quite rise to the challenge. For instance, if you're working with a twenties theme, an old fedora, a cigar, or a flapper-style beaded necklace will help the less sartorially inclined.

If you can't afford an acting troupe and don't want to buy a prepackaged game, look to your favorite old mystery novel and develop a storyline on your own (just make sure it's a book your guests haven't read). But don't stress over the preparations. These parties should be fun for everyone, including the host.

THE PARTY

You want to keep the party fun and active throughout the night so you don't lose everybody's interest. That's why Bridget added a scavenger hunt to both her parties. She wanted the party to be very *Clue*-like, which makes participation really important. "You have to keep it going," Bridget warns. "Because parties like that can get into a lull when everybody goes, 'Oh, never mind. Let's just have some more cocktails and forget about it.'" Having somebody there to

coordinate things, whether it's an acting troupe or a friend or just you, make sure someone knows what the next thing is to do and how to keep people motivated and moving.

THE MENU

The food should also fit in with the theme, no matter what time period your party takes place. Bridget did research on Los Angeles in the twenties and thirties and learned that Chinese food was very popular during that time. "So I made sure my menu was completely Chinese-themed," she explains. "We even did fortune cookies that had a special message pertaining to the party inside of them and gave a clue. You can do that kind of thing with any time period. If you set a specific era for the party, you should research it online and find out what kind of clothes they wore, what kind of food they liked to eat, what was popular, what was in style. Everything."

Halloween
Pumpkin-Carving Party

HALLOWEEN BRINGS ONE of the biggest annual parties at the Mansion, but the Girls have almost as much fun in the lead-up to the holiday as at the party itself, preparing for it with a pumpkin-carving night.

SETUP

A pumpkin-carving party can get very messy. The first thing you need to do is lay down as much plastic sheeting as you can to cover the floor and table. You'll also need big bowls for the pumpkin innards and paper towels for cleanup.

There are some helpful carving kits available, but you'll want to buy extra since, as the Girls learned firsthand, the plastic knives have a tendency to break. There are also battery-operated electric knives that you can use that whip through pumpkins fast. Having the right tools is really important; otherwise you'll be up all night carving. Many of these kits will come with stencils, but don't be afraid to go free-form and design your pumpkin on your own. Just be sure to plot out your cuts first, or your football could turn into a very large mouth. Just ask Kendra.

Costumes are always fun, but don't wear anything for pumpkin carving that could get in the way of the process. And remember, it's a messy event, so it would be best to leave the vintage wardrobe in the closet.

DECORATIONS

Y ou should start with the table and work your way out, since that's the focal point of the night. Black plastic sheeting will protect your table from the mess, and it makes a good foundation for your décor. Throw a plastic table runner down the middle and go to town. Party stores have aisles full of decorations in the months leading up to Halloween, so there's no excuse for a bare room. Of course, the truly committed will travel to Halloween conventions and get the good stuff before it's available to the public.

For ambiance, freaky music is a must. You can do fun Halloween music, like "Monster Mash" and "Dead Man's Party" and that kind of stuff, but Bridget also recommends Midnight Syndicate creepy music (www.midnightsyndicate.com).

MENU

A s with any gathering, food is an important component. Set out snacks along a second table so pumpkin innards don't get mixed in. Creating a menu with fun names for everyday snacks is also a good way to turn traditional staples into creative—and gruesome—delicacies. Pigs in a blanket are fun, but imagine your guests' reactions when you hand them severed toes with ketchup blood. On the opposite page is the menu from the Girls' pumpkin-carving night.

Pumpkin Night

SHIT ON A SHINGLE **Refried Beans, Cheddar Cheese, Fresh Corn Chips**

TOES IN A BLANKET **Weenie Roll-Ups**

ROADKILL PIZZA **Tomato, Black Olives, Pepperoncini, Mozzarella Cheese**

TACO HELL **Seasoned Beef, Lettuce, Tomato, Cheddar Cheese, Crunchy Corn Shells**

COMPOST PILE **Olive Garden Salad**

SNOTTY SALAD **Caesar Salad**

DESSERT: **LITTER-BOX CAKE**

Baby Shower

THERE ISN'T OFTEN cause to throw a baby shower at the Mansion, so when Playmate Victoria Fuller announced she was expecting, Holly went all out hosting a baby shower at the Playmate house to celebrate the joyous occasion.

PARTY PREP

Baby showers are a girl thing. You don't need boys—like the husband—to help with the planning, although you can invite them to stop by later for cake (since somebody needs to carry the gifts home).

You can get traditional pastel decorations at any party store, but why not be creative? Since this party is all about the mommy-to-be, the theme can be, too. Like Holly did, you can take things from the expectant mom's life—photos, mementos, pop artwork—and use them as decorations. Laurie Rodgers, the Mansion Pastry Chef, whipped up a cake with a childhood photo of Victoria in the center. This is something a lot of bakeries and supermarkets can do, too.

GIFT-GIVING

Remember that the guest of honor is *pregnant*. When it's time to open the gifts, bring the presents to her, don't make her go to them (especially if there are heavy ones). Presents should be for the baby, but they can also be all about you—give a gift that reflects your personality. Whether it's a tomboy sports pack, a bunny collection, or your favorite Dr. Seuss book, this is your chance to influence a new life. As far as Holly's concerned, "Bringing interesting gifts and watching the guest of honor open the gifts is the best part of the party."

THE POOPIE-DIAPER GAME

Party games are a must. Here's a fun one that Bridget taught Holly for the shower.

ITEMS REQUIRED
Assorted candy bars
Clean diapers
Marker
Notepad

1 Use the marker to number each of the diapers. You will need as many diapers as you have candy bars (and maybe an extra few, in case of accidents).

2 Melt the candy bars and spread each into a clean diaper, making a note of which candy bar is in which numbered diaper.

3 Bring out the dirty diapers and have fun watching your guests try to figure out the diaper contents by smelling, touching, and maybe even tasting the assorted candy bars.

NAME THE BABY FOOD

This game is similar in concept to the Poopie-Diaper Game. All this one requires is jars of baby food and spoons. Remove the labels from the jars and hand out spoons to your guests. The object is to guess the identity of the baby food in the jar by any means necessary.

Season 2

Here's Looking at You, Hef

It's Hef's eightieth birthday weekend and everyone gets dolled up, forties-style, to open the festivities with Casablanca Night. Holly presents Hef with a pair of white peacocks, like the ones that used to be part of the Mansion zoo. Kendra has a special *Playboy Mansion Confidential* noir poster made for Hef, and Bridget prepares a special birthday treat for the big bash by rehearsing a striptease for her man.

Bridget: Jumping out of that cake was huge for me. That was really taking myself out of my comfort zone. Even though I'd posed for the magazine before, doing that kind of routine was really so liberating. It's very empowering. I feel like it advanced me to a whole other level of comfort with myself. I still look back on that as one of my favorite memories of my time here.

Eighty Is the New Forty

Hef continues his eightieth-birthday celebration with a small party in the backyard for a thousand of his closest friends. But *this* soiree isn't forties-style elegance; the dress code is lingerie or less—a fact that concerns Kendra, whose mother is on the guest list. During the party, Bridget springs her striptease gift on Hef by popping out of a cake. Holly also hosts a lunch for the Playmates from the seventies who came in for the party.

Holly: [Hef's former social secretary] Alison Reynolds has a reunion every year with her best friends, a bunch of Playmates from the seventies. So I decided to help her host one of the luncheons. It was really fun to hear all the old stories and see all the old pictures. Playmates back then have a lot of the same bond as Playmates today. It made me look forward to the days in the future when I'm older and having reunions with all my friends.

Career Dazed

The Girls film a cameo in *Scary Movie 4* and explore the career opportunities their success has brought. They also enjoy the perks of celebrity when Bridget borrows a Porsche that she ultimately gets to keep and Kendra has a grill made to celebrate her graduating from massage-therapy school. Meanwhile, Captain Morgan wants to do an ad with Holly and Bridget that Kendra can't be in because she's too young to appear in alcohol advertisements. Kendra shoots a cover for *MuscleMag* instead.

Kendra: Sometimes we're in a movie or shows and the producers or the writers want us just because we're the three blondes. But our show should have shown already that that's not all we are. People see us on the show, and then they see us in a movie acting totally different. Our fans know who we are, and they're like, "Wait a minute. That's not how Kendra acts. If they're going to have those three in the movie, they might as well have them be themselves."

PLAYBOY

E RETURN OF THE GIRLS NEXT DOOR

www.playboy.com • SEPTEMBER 2006

ENTERTAINMENT FOR MEN

EXPLOSIVE INTERVIEW: EX-FEMA BOSS MICHAEL BROWN •
EVA LONGORIA SEXES UP 20Q • JOURNEY TO THE CENTER
OF A COAL MINE • PARIS HILTON'S LOOK-ALIKE NUDE •
WORLD'S BEST COLLEGE FOOTBALL PICKS • SMART FASHION

THE VOLKSWAGEN RABBIT. IT'S BACK.

www.playboy.com • SEPTEMBER 2006

ENTERTAINMENT FOR MEN

Mutiny on the Booty

The Girls prepare for their second *Playboy* photo shoot, but
they aren't crazy about the setup on Hef's famous round bed.
They suggest their own photos that reflect their individual per-
sonalities to make it different from the first shoot, which was all
about the trio. But the unprecedented two-sided photo that will
appear on both the front and back covers causes some strife.

*Holly: My favorite cover is the second one, because it was
the first front-and-back cover Playboy ever did. Also, it was my idea.
We were at a Dodgers game and we were trying to think of a cover. I
took a Sharpie and, on a napkin, I drew us undressing through a window like a neighbor was looking at us: The Girls Next Door. The napkin
is so ugly. It doesn't make any sense, but Hef liked it. He sent it off to
Chicago, and it became the cover.*

PLAYBOY

TAKE A
PEEK AT...
THE
GIRLS
NEXT
DOOR

San Diego or Bust

Kendra takes Hef, Holly, and Bridget to visit her hometown, where her mom has been doing some serious cleaning for the special visit. A *Playboy*-themed train carries them down the coast for lunch and an afternoon of sightseeing.

Kendra: My mom was the most nervous person you'll ever meet that day. She was so nervous because Hugh Hefner was coming to our little house in Clairemont. We're in Clairemont. Come on, it's weird! All my brother's friends had to see it for themselves. It was really special that Hef came down to visit.

Heavy Petting

Springtime at the Mansion brings the birth of many new baby animals, the annual family Easter party, and a birthday party for Wednesday. But all the family fun just reminds Holly that she and Hef still don't have any little ones of their own . . . yet.

Bridget: I knew I wanted a birthday cake for the dogs. Three Dog Bakery (www.threedog .com) was cool. They have all different kinds of cookies and treats. People can eat them, too. We tried them. The cookies are like little Oreos, and they're actually good. They gave me one and I was like, "Yum!" eating it on my way home.

123

Sleepwear Optional

In the lead-up to the Playmate of the Year luncheon, Holly throws a slumber party in honor of the 2006 Playmate of the Year, Kara Monaco. She also starts a new tradition of giving the Playmate of the Year a necklace she designed herself.

Holly: We have a traditional Playmate necklace that Hef gives to every girl when the Centerfold comes out, but I thought the Playmate of the Year should have a special one. I wanted it to be diamonds with a pink sapphire eye and a bow tie, because pink is traditionally the Playmate of the Year color. I also wanted it to be bigger than the Playmate necklace so it stands out a little bit more.

I See London, I See France

The celebration of Hef's eightieth-birthday year continues with the first leg of a European trip with the Girls. The paparazzi are out in force as they tour England and France with an itinerary that is jam-packed with sightseeing and partying.

Bridget on traveling with Hef: It is a major undertaking. It's crazy. It's unheard-of preparation. First of all, it has to be a private jet. It has to be first-class accommodations. And not just one hotel room—it has to be the giant suite. We take over almost a whole wing sometimes, or a whole floor of certain hotels, depending on how big they are. At least entire sections, because we travel with security and assistants and, of course, all us girls and usually Hef's brother, and tour guides and PR, and when the camera crew comes with us . . . It's just an insane entourage. Not to mention the preparation that goes into it. Everything *has* to be planned. It's an itinerary that keeps us constantly on the run.

When in Rome

The European tour moves on to Spain, Germany, and Italy. Hef and the Girls encounter a rather determined paparazzo in Venice, but the photographer doesn't manage to spoil the romantic gondola ride that closes out their trip.

Bridget: Italy was my favorite place that we went to. Ever since I learned about Pompeii in my Western Civilization class, I've always wanted to go there. I never even really thought it would ever come to fruition. Growing up, traveling outside the United States seemed like such a wild and crazy thing that I might never get to do in my life. So to go there and actually go to Pompeii was amazing for me. That was my favorite trip. Plus, I just love Italy—Rome, Venice, all of it.

Baby Talk

Holly hosts a baby shower for expectant Playmate Victoria Fuller. Kendra deals with a rogue wasp in her bedroom and helps with one of the Mansion's many prank calls. Bridget has Gizmo's teeth cleaned. None of these things are as simple as they seem . . . well, except the prank call. Kendra puts an end to *that* with a "kindly suggestion" and a hang-up.

Holly: The baby shower was a challenge for me because I had never been to a baby shower before. Bridget was kind enough to give me some ideas for really fun, gross games, like the Poopie-Diaper Game. I think the shock value of that game kind of carried the whole party. It was certainly memorable.

The 21 Club

The Girls celebrate Kendra's twenty-first birthday in Vegas with a rare—past curfew—overnight bacchanal, but the party is nearly ruined when she has trouble finding her grill. All is well once it's located, and Don "Magic" Juan gifts her with a special pimp cup to go with it. For a more relaxed celebration, Kendra's mom, grandmother, and brother come to Los Angeles for dinner with their extended family.

Kendra: Everybody has to celebrate their twenty-first birthday in Vegas. I went there and I went buck wild. There are so many things that you didn't even see on the show. They don't even put any of that good stuff on the DVDs. Too bad!

Girls Will Be Ghouls

Getting in the Halloween spirit, Bridget conducts her own paranormal investigation of the Mansion and takes a tour of haunted Hollywood. The Girls host a pumpkin-carving night with some of the Playmates, and the Mansion celebrates the annual Halloween party and haunted house. Even Bridget's car gets into costume, with new Playboy-style rims.

Bridget: When we went and saw where the Black Dahlia body was found, I just had to have my picture taken there, even though it was somebody's front lawn. I was a little embarrassed about it, but I just thought, "This is a once-in-a-lifetime chance. I'm just going to do it." Hopefully the people who live in that house weren't home. Or they were probably looking out their window, saying, "What the hell are these girls doing? Get the shotgun!"

The Age of Aquarium

Love is in the air as Hef and Holly celebrate their fifth anniversary. Holly gifts her man with new tropical fish for the tanks in the aviary. The staff turns the living room into Hef's Melting Pot for an anniversary fondue dinner for the pair. The Girls also appear on the *Loveline* radio show. But all is not hearts and flowers when Kendra posts a blog about a mishap at a rap video shoot, which makes news on entertainment Web sites, prompting the staff to do some damage control.

Holly on her fondness for fondue: It all started with a surprise party Bridget threw for me for my birthday a couple years before. She asked Hank [Fawcett] to make tables with little burners like at the Melting Pot, one of my favorite restaurants. Then the staff went and got the actual pots from the restaurant, and all the recipes and stuff. Our anniversary was the second time we did it, so they've gotten really good at re-creating the Melting Pot at home.

Rabbit Season

The Girls help interview Bunny candidates for the new Playboy Club at the Palms. Even though it's suggested that Holly *not* wear her Bunny outfit for the interviews, she can't keep her inner Bunny at bay and rebels, sporting her specially made costume. From a pool of three hundred girls, they cull the list down to about twenty potential Bunnies for Hef and Palms owner George Maloof to make their final selection.

Kendra: I don't wear the Bunny costume because it's really uncomfortable on me. That doesn't mean I don't respect Playboy. *I love* Playboy. *I love the history and all that. But it's just not my thing to wear a Bunny costume. I'm not a Bunny, so it doesn't feel natural.*

We Can Work It Out

Bridget and Holly have some concerns over the their intense diet and exercise regimen while preparing to shoot their very own workout DVD. None of the Girls wants to give a false impression of who they are for their viewers. Sporty Kendra is most excited about the shoot, but stresses on the day of the taping. The Girls take an exercise break with Hef when they go to see Playmate and actress Julie McCullough perform stand-up at the Improv.

Kendra's most important workout tip: Have fun. If you don't have fun, you're just going to get bored and not want to do it. Working out should not be torture. Working out should be something you want to do. So you need to find something you want to do. Anything: hiking, biking, rock climbing. Anything that makes you happy. If you're stuck on a treadmill every day and you hate it, you're eventually going to quit because it's torture. Who wants to torture themselves? So do something that makes you happy.

Playboys After Dark

The Playboy Club makes a triumphant return with the opening of the new venue at the Palms Hotel in Las Vegas. Kendra visits her uncle, who used to work at the Playboy Club in Atlantic City and is now staffed at the Palms. Bridget works as a special correspondent for *Extra*, and the Girls and Hef have a calendar signing at the Playboy Store. But nothing beats all the revelry surrounding the grand opening.

Hef: The return of the Bunny is a dream come true for me. Everything is timing. There was a period of time in which Playboy—the brand, and certainly the Bunnies—was considered rather old-fashioned. Certainly the Bunnies were, when the Playboy Clubs closed following the loss of our casino licenses in England in the early eighties. But a moment came when—and it's impossible to separate it from my own reemergence after the marriage—the Playboy brand became hot again. If we had opened the Playboy Club Casino in the early 1990s, I don't think it would be doing at all what it is doing now. We reached a point in which a whole generation had grown up not only waiting for me to come out and play, but a whole generation had grown up in the eighties and nineties and felt as if they had missed the party in the sixties and seventies. All of a sudden Playboy and retro cool seemed very romantic. I think that's what the Bunnies are all about. I think it's part of a retro-cool phenomenon.

How to Look Like a Playmate

1. Lipstick is not really necessary if you have a good **LIP LINER** and gloss. It's good to have three shades you're in love with: a neutral, a pink, and a red. Mine are Playboy Beauty's lip liners In the Buff, Mauvelous, and Crimson Kisses. My favorite lip glosses are Playboy Beauty's Centerfold Red, Bobbi Brown's Petal, and MAC's Clear Lipglass.

2. Paula Dorf's **ENHANCER** in Baby Eyes is great for camouflaging blemishes.

3. My favorite **BRONZER** is Guerlain's Terracotta. Be sure you have a special brush for your bronzer.

4. I have really oily skin, so I use MAC **BLOT FILM** throughout the day in addition to powder.

5. For a **NATURAL LOOK**, stick to tinted moisturizer, mascara, blush, and a light lip gloss, like Playboy Beauty's Mood lip gloss.

6. Everyone's face is different. Since I have large features, I need to enhance my brows and lashes for balance. If I am getting really made-up, I always use **FALSE EYELASHES** and draw in my eyebrows.

7. My favorite **BLUSH** is Playboy Beauty's Cabana Boy. It would definitely be one of the things I would take to a deserted island.

8. I always have major red-eye, and I'm not even drunk or high! I use the blue **EYE DROPS** from France. Visine doesn't even work on me!

9. I love Cinema Secrets **FOUNDATION**. It's oil-free, so it won't make you break out.

10. I always use black mascara and eyeliner, if I wear any at all. As for eye shadow, I like white on my brow bone, orange in the creases of my eyelids, and brown in the corners of my eyelids to create a **CAT-EYE EFFECT**.

BRIDGET'S TIPS FOR HEALTHY LIVING . . .

1. My number one rule for healthy living is just feeling comfortable with who you are. If you're **COMFORTABLE WITH YOURSELF** and your body, everything else will fall into place.

2. My diet is all about **MODERATION**. Never deny yourself that piece of birthday cake—just don't overdo it . . . and know you might have to work it off later.

3. **PETS** aren't only great companions, but they're good for exercise and de-stressing. Wednesday is my reason to get out of bed in the morning because when she has to move, I do, too. Winnie and Gizmo are also great to curl up with in bed and relax together after a hard day.

4. The one thing I always carry with me is **LIP GLOSS** because I hate dry lips. I mostly use MAC lip gloss. It doesn't matter if it's colored or clear. I just need something on my lips.

5. To keep my skin moisturized, I put a little **VASELINE** under my eyes and on my hands at night.

. . . AND FABULOUS HAIR

1. I use Frederic Fekkai shampoo and conditioner. If you're blond, they have this stuff called Baby Blonde that helps neutralize the color. I also use their Glossing Shampoo, mostly because I love the smell, but what girl can't use a little more **SHINE** in her hair?

2. I also use Protein RX shampoo and I **TAKE TURNS** with these, depending on what I feel like I need at the time. But you can't use that all the time—just a couple times a week.

3. I know scrunchies are taboo, but I'm not embarrassed to throw my hair in a ball on top of my head and run out the door with a **SCRUNCHIE** if I'm really in a hurry and not going anywhere special.

4. I love **HAIR EXTENSIONS**. I've tried a lot of different kinds. I've had the individuals, but they really ruined my hair. So you have to be really careful with those. Now I have the rows in, and they are awesome. You take them out and there's little to no damage. It depends on who you have do them—you want to make sure you go to somebody really, really good.

5. Clip-in extensions are equally good. For the longest time I used **CLIP-IN EXTENSIONS**. You can take them out when you go to bed at night. They don't ruin your hair. So I highly recommend clip-in extensions as well.

KENDRIQUETTE LESSONS

Who needs etiquette lessons? Just be yourself. It should all come naturally for the environment you're in. If you're with people you grew up with and you eat sloppy, then eat sloppy. It all depends on the situation. Etiquette lessons didn't do anything for me, because I will forever do what I want to do. I'm a rebel. And this is how I roll . . .

To practice good posture, walk while balancing a book on your head.

You can't shake your ass with a book on your head. Well, you can, but it takes a lot of practice.

A lady should never cuss.

Sometimes a good cuss at the right time can help you express yourself.

Saying "Hello" is better than "Yo!"

Yeah, my friends wouldn't know what to say if I came up to them being all,
"Hello, how are you this fine day?" Just be real. If you feel like saying "Yo!" say "Yo!"

There are a number of rules for the proper handling and use of a fork while dining.

Screw that! You don't need a fork to eat fried chicken.

Never lick your fingers while eating. Always use a napkin.

Hello! Why do you think they call it "finger-lickin' good"?

Never make "mmmm" sounds at the dinner table. Compliment the host on a fine meal instead.

When I'm saying "mmmmm," it means I really like the food. That's a natural reaction.
And I thought you weren't supposed to talk with your mouth full.

Never lick a butter knife clean.

I say, "Waste not, want not." Besides, you don't want to mess up the tablecloth when you put
your knife back down, do you?

If you need to use the restroom, simply say, "Excuse me, I'll be right back."
No need to share too much information.

What's wrong with being honest? Everybody shits. Nothing wrong with telling people you have to go.

One should refrain from getting excessively drunk.
That is when all sorts of behavior can happen to make others uncomfortable.

That's kind of the point of getting drunk!

A true lady should not drink from a pimp cup.

She should if it's got her beer in it!

The Girls Next Door Makeover

THE *PLAYBOY* IMAGE of the Girl Next Door has always been an understated beauty: a natural, everyday woman. But even Playmates have to get done up when they hit the town. Natural beauty takes a lot of work these days, as the show's audience witnessed in the first-season episode, "Midsummer Night's Dream," when Bridget, Holly, and Kendra took an everyday beautiful girl next door, Bridget's sister, Anastasia Case, and dolled her up Playmate-style. It was a chance for Bridget to re-create her days playing dress-up with her little sister, but now for all the world to see. 🐰 ANASTASIA'S MAKEOVER FOR the Midsummer Night's Dream party was a total surprise for her, and a welcome relief when she found out what had been going on. "I remember Bridget would leave the room for two hours at a time at night to go talk to Kendra and Holly down the hallway," Anastasia says. "I felt really left out, actually. I remember talking to my mom, saying, 'I just feel left out. Bridget's very secretive right now.' All along, my mom knew. She's like, 'It's okay.'" And everything did turn out okay. Even though Anastasia had been spending her summer at the Mansion, she wasn't technically a part of the production, so she was shocked, thrilled, and maybe even a little confused to find that they were devoting an episode to her. 🐰 THE MAKEOVER WAS condensed into one episode, but the actual party prep took more than two weeks of spa treatments,

waxing, and spray tans, and at least one slap on the ass. Though some of it was a relaxing vacation, a lot of it was work . . . and maybe even a little punishment. The end results were stunning, giving Anastasia a whole new look so that even Hef didn't recognize her. 🐰 **HERE ARE SOME** of the highlights of her makeover that took her all around the Los Angeles area.

SKIN SPA
17401 Ventura Blvd., Encino
www.skinspa.com

The spa owned by Jonathan Baker (husband of January 1996 Playmate Victoria Fuller) offered a full-day treatment for Anastasia and her sister. "It was everything," Anastasia recalls. "It was a full-on massage and facial, and we also did this thing where they scrub you down—your whole body is naked—and there's like a rain shower in there coming down. It's supposed to exfoliate your body. And then there was the manicure, pedicure, lunch."

PINK CHEEKS
14562 Ventura Blvd., Sherman Oaks
www.pinkcheeks.com

Next Holly took Anastasia to Pink Cheeks for a bikini wax in front of the cameras. Although she had already had her body exfoliating filmed, Anastasia was wondering how the whole waxing thing was going to work with a cameraman in the room. She was reassured that they'd only film her legs, and then from the waist up, but even so, Anastasia came prepared. "My sister was mortified that I was wearing granny panties. But when the camera is on your butt, you don't want to be wearing a G-string. That's what Holly told Bridget. She goes, 'At least your sister wasn't wearing a G-string.' And to have the woman slap me on the ass! I don't really know what that was about."

CLAIRE PETTIBONE BOUTIQUE
236 S. Robertson Blvd., Beverly Hills
www.clairepettibone.com

VICTORIA'S SECRET
www.victoriassecret.com

Of course, an important component in getting ready for a party that's billed as "lingerie or less" would have to be finding the perfect outfit. Anastasia may have had something already in mind from Victoria's Secret, but when filming restrictions kept the show from taping her at the store, it just meant that she and Bridget had to make another shopping trip to Claire Pettibone Boutique. In the end, she went with her original outfit, but even that had its problems. "The night of the party, there was another girl wearing the exact same outfit. I was like, 'What the . . . !' But Bridget told me, 'Well, it *is* Victoria's Secret. You kind of have to expect that a thousand other girls are going to be wearing that.'"

JOSÉ EBER SALON

224 North Rodeo Dr., Beverly Hills

www.joseeberatelier.com

The most stunning part of the transformation came in Anastasia's makeup and hair, as overseen by some-one already familiar to the *Girls Next Door* audience. "Laurent had done my hair a couple of times, but nothing like this," says Anastasia. "I had like short, brown, curly hair. I would go with Bridget, and she would get her hair done for like four hours. She would have to be double-processed, hair bleached blond and color on top of that, with highlights and a blow-out. So getting my hair done was—by far, out of everything that happened—the best gift the show could have given me. That was the one thing that really transformed me."

The Girls Next Door
Posing Tips

Holly: Everybody's so different that you just have to study your own pictures and realize what looks good and what doesn't. Mix up your facial expressions. Practice in the mirror. Move every time the camera clicks.

Bridget: Suck in your stomach, stick out your butt, and smile. Have a good time and just smile. Laugh. That's my look, and that's what I go for. At the same time, I have to remember to suck in my stomach and push out my butt because that evens out the back of your legs and makes your butt look good.

Kendra: When you suck in your gut, don't make a face. You have to lose your gut, but don't make that face like you're trying to suck in. I made a couple of mistakes on that and I'm like, "Never again." You just have to learn how to suck your gut in and breathe at the same time.

Season 3

❦ Snow Place Like Home ❦

Snow day at the Mansion! In honor of the holidays, Hef lets Holly and Bridget hire a snowmaker to coat the backyard for some winter fun. But that's not the only surprise, as the Girls wrap their Christmas presents for one another and for a family in need. Even the animals get into the act when Bridget invites a pet chef over to teach her to make holiday treats.

Bridget: Having the snow here was awesome. I tried to do it for Holly's birthday one year because we really wanted to go sledding, but it was too expensive. But then we got to do it for Christmas the next year, which was awesome. We originally wanted to do it on the hill at the side of the house, but that's really dangerous—there's no way to stop. The guys looked at that and they were like, "Oh, you're crazy. You'll never stop. You'll kill yourself." So we put hay bales on the front lawn to make smaller hills, and we had a blast.

May the Horse Be with You

The Girls ring in 2007 at the Mansion's annual New Year's Eve party and make a trio of resolutions. Holly promises to do more with the Playmates and organizes an outing to go horseback riding. Bridget focuses on her career by starting work on her demo reel. And Kendra gets some help from Julie McCullough in trying to fulfill her goal to get organized—but first she has to get out of bed.

Kendra: I don't wake up for just anything. If it's something I love doing, like snowboarding or something, I'll get up. BAM! I'll be up. But other times it's kind of difficult. This didn't just start now. It was hard for me to get up for high school in San Diego. It was so hard for me to wake up. I couldn't do it. Waking up is probably the hardest part of my day.

Let Them Eat Birthday Cake

Holly celebrates her twenty-seventh birthday with a Marie Antoinette–themed party at the Mansion. The guests are done up in period garb, and even the staff gets in on the costume theme. As a gift, Hef gives Holly a golf cart that Bridget has had customized, Playboy-style.

Holly: That was my favorite birthday ever! I'm obsessed with Marie Antoinette and Versailles. The movie [Sofia Coppola's Marie Antoinette] had just come out that year, and I wanted to do a party that was themed after the movie. I dressed all my friends up and orchestrated the decorations and the menu, which I filled with the best desserts: a chocolate mousse and strawberry shortcake and different kinds of petit fours. We had broccoli cheese crepes and steak and little mini ham-and-cheese sandwiches and shrimp cocktail. It was all my favorite foods.

My Bare Lady

Attending a showing of the Playboy Legacy Collection inspires Holly to take a job as an apprentice editor. She works with West Coast Editor Marilyn Grabowski on a *Playboy* photo shoot, learning from the expert how to create a Centerfold. Also interested in investing in their futures, Kendra looks into some real estate and Bridget continues her work on her demo reel.

Holly on her current role at Playboy Studio West: I kind of took over the whole production for the Playmate feature, which is in every magazine. I start by looking for girls, testing girls, orchestrating their shoots, and coming up with the themes. I'm there on the day of the shoots, supervising everything. I edit the photos and layouts, and I catalog all the pictures because you have to get a lot of content on each girl. It's a lot of work, but I love it. My favorite pictorial is still the first one I did, with Tamara Sky.

⌐ Calendar Girls ⌐

The Girls pose for their 2008 calendar, each posing in individual shots designed to match her personality. Holly oversees the shoot, but she prefers not to make a big deal about it around Hef for fear of him getting too involved.

Bridget on her bewitching calendar pose: It was difficult. Basically, I was trying to hold myself up on a two-by-four at an angle. At first there was nothing to put my foot on. I had on these big black boots that came to a point. I was trying to hold on with one toe and stabilize myself on there because there was nothing on either side of me. And I couldn't use my hands because I had to hold on to the broom. On top of all that, I had to smile and try to look sexy at the same time. Finally, they pounded on a little piece of wood for my toe to hit on, but still I was basically holding up my entire weight and trying to balance on a toe and a knee.

Snowboarded

The Girls get styled up in winter gear and head to Vail, Colorado, for some snowboarding with Olympian Shaun White. While they hit the slopes, relax with massages, and chow down on elk, Hef keeps himself entertained back at the Mansion, hosting a card night for the guys.

Kendra on snowboarding with Shaun White: It was the last run of the day and I told him, "This is it. I want to race you. I just want to fly with you." And he was like, "All right." So we fly down the hill, like seriously fly. I'm keeping up with him. He's going off these little branches and I'm staying right with him. Of course, he's going off the big jumps, flipping and shit. I'm like, "Uh . . . no." But I'm still flying. There's a part where I actually got in front of him. It was cool. I will forever have these memories to tell my kids about. These are legends. They're not just regular snowboarders or surfers or whatever. They're legends.

Hearts Afire

Valentine's Day at the Mansion is celebrated with a gift exchange that is on fire . . . largely due to a minor gift wrap/candle mishap. The holiday of love is celebrated throughout the Mansion, with even Duke and Winnie getting in on the action, celebrating their burgeoning relationship with a romantic carriage ride . . . in Holly's golf cart. But all is not just hearts and flowers, as the Mansion's occupants party hard for Mardi Gras.

Holly on her outfit, which became the inspiration for the Peacock Painted Lady: My favorite outfit is definitely the peacock outfit. Trashy Lingerie had made a flamingo one, and I told them, "I want to be a peacock." I collected a bunch of peacock feathers from around the Mansion and worked with them selecting the fabrics. Then I rhinestoned it myself. It turned out really nice.

PMOY Not?

It's time to vote for Playmate of the Year, which is particularly difficult since the Girls are friends with several of the candidates. Holly, Bridget, and Kendra each take out the girls living in the Playmate House for an afternoon of fun, ranging from a German dinner to a trip to the driving range to revisiting past employment with a meal at Hooters. Based on the readers' votes and Hef's opinion, Sara Underwood is ultimately named Playmate of the Year.

Holly: I loved working at Hooters because if you're going to be a waitress, you might as well be a waitress somewhere fun. They encourage you to have fun with the guests. Sit down, show them card tricks, and hula hoop and roller-skate and do all kinds of fun things. Roller skating was my favorite part; I could exercise while I worked. And I would carry plates of food on my head. I was really good at it.

Family Affairs

Holly produces a photo shoot, while Kendra enlists her family to help fix up her new condo. Bridget hits Chicago with her mom for the annual Halloween convention.

Bridget on her Halloween obsession: All I can attribute it to is my love for the scary-movie genre. At a young age, my mom would let me rent horror movies. The most fun thing for me to do was have my cousins over, and we would rent scary movies—like five of them—and try to stay up all night long, eating junk food, drinking Kool-Aid, and watching scary movies and scaring ourselves. That was our favorite thing to do.

Home, Sweet Suite

Hef celebrates his eighty-first birthday in Vegas, which is more than enough reason for the Girls to go on a shopping spree to find the perfect outfits for partying. While they're right at home in the Hugh Hefner Sky Villa at the Palms, they are also happy to head back to the Mansion in time for Casablanca Night.

Kendra: My favorite part of the Hugh Hefner Sky Villa is the pool overlooking the city. It looks like it just goes right over the edge. I love that pool. I have a lot of fun in that pool. That thing is my favorite. And then, of course, there's the elevator. I love the details like that; the elevator and stuff that's not in a normal hotel room. I also love how it's all done up with Playboy decorations. You know from the moment you walk in that this is Playboy.

blue-green with black lace pattern on top

lace top v-neus

Bedtime Stories: The Best of the Girls Next Door

Hef and the Girls curl up in bed for a special episode where they recall some of their favorite (and not-so-favorite) moments so far.

Training Dazed

Kendra learns some etiquette, while Bridget brings in a dog trainer to help teach Winnie some new tricks. Holly continues to pursue her career as a photo editor, taking a trip to Vegas to apprentice on a shoot for a Playboy Bunny pictorial. But she's not the only one with a job—even Winnie has a career, as cohost of *The Bridget & Wednesday Friday Show* on the Playboy station on Sirius Radio.

Kendra: There were certain reasons why I wanted to take etiquette lessons. And it wasn't about figuring out the right fork to use. The whole point of the etiquette lessons was because we were about to go to Monte Carlo to see the prince. I just wanted to be a little more comfortable with things, not change who I am. I just wanted to learn things like the proper way to shake a hand. Just to reassure me of posture and stuff. That's why I was kind of annoyed when she wanted me to do the fork thing. I didn't care about that.

Dangerous Curves

The Girls are in the drivers' seats when Kendra races in the Toyota Pro-Celebrity Race. Holly leases an energy-efficient car and designs the decals to pimp it out. And Bridget picks up her customized Playboy rims and unveils them in a cover shoot for *Lexani Lifestyle* magazine.

Kendra: During the qualifying race the day before, I was like the only one who didn't crash. The only one! I did great and I was all ready to go. I was like, "Man, everybody's going to crash. I'm going to be the one to win." That's what I was hoping. So it came down to the race and I was doing so good and then I think someone did something to my tires. They cheated! *I'm kidding. I think I just passed John Salley or someone. I passed them right before a turn. I just got too cocky and I ran into the wall.*

Surely, You Joust

Hef and the Girls visit a Renaissance Faire. But first, Bridget helps Kendra find the perfect outfit, and she has a language coach come in to teach proper faire speak. Holly has a costume specially made to resemble the dress of Disney's Sleeping Beauty, and even Hef gets into the act, attending as the King of France.

Bridget on the Renaissance Faire life: It started out for me when my aunt worked it in Northern California. I used to work the faire with her. The one in Novato, at the Black Point Forest, was the coolest faire ever. I used to work it year after year after year. When I came to L.A., my friend Stacy was like, "Oh my god, I go to the Renaissance Pleasure Faire here every year!" Well, I'd never been to the Southern California one before. So we just started going every year. Finally, last year, I talked Holly and Hef into it and dragged Kendra along.

Guess Who's Coming to Luncheon?

Holly welcomes her family *and* Barbi Benton to the events surrounding the Playmate of the Year luncheon. The Girls have a star named in Playmate of the Year Sara Underwood's honor, and everyone hits the town to celebrate.

Hef: What's set the Playmates apart from the beginning was that they were not simply glamour girls. They were not simply the sophisticated girls from New York or Los Angeles. They were the girl next door. And that concept started very, very early. The first girl next door was somebody who actually worked for the magazine named Janet Pilgrim. And we promoted that as the concept and invented the foldout Centerfold, which became iconic. But I would say that it's all about natural beauty. And that's what sets them apart. I think the same thing is true, of course, for the show, and it's true for my own personal taste. My own personal taste and my life are never far apart from the magazine.

Lingerie or Less ...the Good, the Bad, and the Naked

Holly on her style . . .

IT VARIES. I would say during the week, when I'm working or just hanging around the house, I'm very casual. Almost a little bit skaterish. I like to wear Converse and tube socks and stuff from Hot Topic.

When I'm dressing up, I like very elegant, classic styles—things that remind me of Marilyn Monroe or Grace Kelly, with a very, very glamorous feel. Then, anytime I have an excuse, I love to go crazy and just wear a really fuckin' fun costume. It could be anything: a really elaborate Marie Antoinette costume, or something really sexy with a random theme, like the peacock costume, or like when we went to New Orleans [in season 5], I wanted to cross-dress, so I dressed up as Criss Angel. So I'm young casual or glamorous or crazy costume. I don't really have one style.

SOME OF HOLLY'S FAVORITE STORES

Victoria's Secret
Hot Topic
Divine Boutique
Just Cavalli

Bridget shares her thoughts on her look . . .

IT'S ABOUT WHERE we're going and what we're doing and the atmosphere around it. If it's Vegas, it's whatever! The sexier the better. If it's dinner, I like to be comfortable and a little more conservative, depending on the restaurant. If we're going to a club in L.A., I try to be very trendy. Something hip. Something new. I try to cater to what I'm going to be doing.

Sometimes I'm really casual, with my hair in a ponytail, no makeup, and tennis shoes. Other days I feel like dressing up in nice jeans and high heels. It depends on my mood when I wake up that day. Sometimes I feel like, "I just want to be comfortable today. I have a million errands to run. I'm going to the car wash and the bank. Who cares?" And then other days I'm like, "You know, I have a million errands to run today. I'm going to the car wash and the bank. Lots of people are out, and I want to look cute and do it all up." It's all about how I feel when I wake up.

A FEW OF BRIDGET'S FAVORITE SHOPS

Marciano

Bebe

Forever 21

Betsey Johnson

Kendra talks K-dub's style . . .

I'M JUST CHILL. It depends on the event. I want to work out every day. Even though I don't work out every day, I always feel like I should if I have a little bit of time. I always dress up in my workout stuff because that's the plan. That way, if I have a little bit of time, I can just run to the gym or go hiking or whatever. If it's a nice event or a party I'll get dressed up. But, you know, sometimes during parties I might not get all done up and formal. I'm just chill. I'm a casual person.

SOME PLACES KENDRA LIKES TO SHOP

Intermix
Target
Niketown
Jimmy Choo

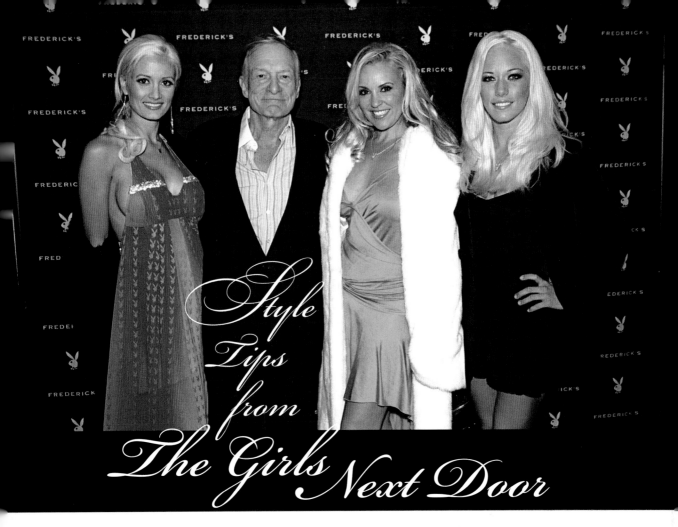

Style Tips from The Girls Next Door

- ▨ Don't mix gold and silver jewelry, and don't over-accessorize. Keep it SIMPLE.

- ▨ Make sure you have a pair of SHOES that you love in gold, silver, black, white, and brown. That should pretty much cover every need.

- ▨ Don't be afraid to have your CLOTHES ALTERED. It makes them look a hundred times better.

- ▨ Have FUN with wearing clothes. Even if you're shy, wearing something outrageous can be a great conversation-starter.

- ▨ Wearing smaller clothing does not make you look skinnier, unless it's a corset. Usually, it just makes you look like a rolled-up sausage.

- ▨ Beware of camel toe and the muffin top. You can wear tight pants, but NOT TOO TIGHT.

- ▨ If you're showing a lot of CLEAVAGE, boob glue or double-stick tape is a must so your dress doesn't fall off, especially if you're going dancing.

- ▨ Make sure you wear PANTIES if you're going to wear a short skirt or dress (especially if you're prone to dancing on couches and tables).

- ▨ Pasties are really helpful if your NIPPLES have a tendency to stick out.

- ▨ There are ways to go trashy, but CLASSY TRASHY. A bra by itself is not stylish, but throw a jacket over it and you just might have something.

Costume Couture

THEY DRESS UP, they dress down, they dress all around. Whether for a "lingerie or less" party or a themed evening of entertainment, The Girls Next Door rely on two L.A. specialty shops for most of their costume needs.

TRASHY LINGERIE
402 N. La Cienega Blvd., Los Angeles
www.trashy.com

Holly and Bridget (and occasionally Kendra) generally have their party outfits made by Trashy Lingerie, the lingerie shop of the stars. Holly shares the process for coming up with some of her signature looks: "I usually come in with a drawing of the outfit I want and I tell them the types of fabric I would like. They tell me what they think would work with it, and then they make it for me. Sometimes I have to compromise because I don't always know how things are made. Or sometimes they won't have the fabric I want. But they've always turned out well. I've always liked what they've done for me. I bet I order something there once a month, or once every other month or so."

REVAMP
834 South Broadway, Suite 1200, Los Angeles
www.revampvintage.com

Whether it's for a Murder Mystery party, Casablanca Night, or some other event with classic themes, Bridget relies on ReVamp for all her vintage needs. She's even become friends with the proprietor, Annamarie, who took Bridget to her very first trapeze lesson. "Annamarie does almost everything I wear that's vintage," Bridget explains. "Or vintage replica, because her specialty is vintage reproductions. She does them for movies and everything.

Mon T-shirt préféré!

My all-time favorite thing to wear is my Fourth of July Bunny costume. It's just so fun!

My Marie Antoinette costume was one of my most elaborate. I love it!

This Bob Mackie one-of-a-kind gown was given to 1979's Playmate of the Year, Monique St. Pierre. I wore it to one of Hef's birthday parties in Vegas.

The Good . . .

This Tinker Bell costume is my favorite of all my Disney Princess costumes.

I loved my Corpse Bride
costume because you
couldn't even tell it
was me.

I love the Bunny suit, period, but the Military Bunny suit is especially wonderful.

Huzzah!

This was my grandma's wedding dress from 1943. It's a perfect dress for Casablanca Night.

To celebrate the Super Bowl, I wore this corset and matching shorts with the *Playboy* number on the back—53, the year the magazine started.

This is my favorite bathing suit.

For the Renaissance Faire I had on these parachute pants and a corset . . . with my LeBron sneakers. That was one of my favorite outfits.

I love wearing anything to do with Chargers gear.

Driving in the Grand Prix was my favorite event ever!

There is no such thing
as too short!

Ewwww!
. . . T.O.!

Bad?
I think I look
adorable!

. . . The Bad . . .

I got this hat in
Saint-Tropez. It
should be on my
worst-dressed
list. . . . But I don't
care! I still love it!

Bridget ✤ Holly ✤ Kendra

... And the Naked!

Season 4

Patriot Dames

Holly is given work space in Hef's personal office in time to take a break for the Fourth of July festivities. This year, they have a custom waterslide made for even wilder backyard fun. In honor of the patriotic holiday, Bridget, Kendra, and some of their Playmate friends attend a farewell party for the Marines who are about to ship out. But while the Marines are heading out, Bridget's brother is coming home on leave and makes a visit to the Mansion.

Kendra: It was great going down there to see the Marines off. I think it was cool that we had the chance to really support them and show them that we're behind them. We come from the same place as most of them, so we know what it's like for them and their families. I'm just glad we could do it.

Heavy Lifting

Holly wants to make over the Mansion's gym, but first she has to convince Hef to let her, which is a daunting task. Kendra's mom comes to L.A. for a makeover of her own and recuperates at the Mansion.

Holly: *The gym is awesome now. I use it so much more than I used to. I love it with the flat-screen TV, and now I have a space for my yoga class. It's a lot more functional now. The whole makeover wasn't so much about changing the look—which I think Hef was really scared of. It was about just about moving a few things around and getting some new pieces of equipment. The function of the place is just so much better now.*

Half-Baked Alaska

Holly takes the Girls to Alaska to see where she grew up. After touring the major metropolis of Ketchikan, they take a floatplane to visit the considerably smaller town of Craig. While in flight, the plane is forced to make an emergency landing, forcing Kendra to face her biggest fear.

Kendra: I always have dreams about that day. First off, I was really afraid of the floatplane from the second I heard we were going on it. And then having to make an emergency landing was the worst feeling ever. I've always had plane crash dreams. So while we were up there, it was like, "Is this it? Is this my dream coming true?" I really cried. There are things you didn't see on TV.

Unveilings

Bridget takes Kendra and friends to a trapeze class for some summertime fun. And the Midsummer Night's Dream party unveils a fresh Arabian Nights theme, as well as a new look for Kendra's mom.

Holly on redesigning their Midsummer Night's Dream seating: I never used to have fun at that party because we would sit on the floor and people would just bombard us all night. Hef would get really tired right away, and really sick of it. He wouldn't have any fun and he would want to go upstairs right away. I always felt like I was working at that party. It was never a fun party for me. So I asked for a tent that kind of sectioned us off a little bit. People could still come up and say hi, but we weren't so out in the open, where people would come up behind us and give us noogies and stuff like they used to.

There's Something About Mary O'Connor

Kendra tees off with other celebrities for the Playboy Golf Scramble, while Holly and Bridget serve as hosts of the event. Hef's personal assistant, Mary, also plays host to the Girls for a night of cards with her friends, while Kendra joins Mary's boyfriend, Captain Bob, for *Monday Night Football*. While the Girls are away, Hef hangs with his friends at his weekly Manly Night. In the end, the Mansion residents and staff gather to surprise Mary on her birthday.

Bridget: Mary is funny. She's kind of the motherly figure here. We all go to her for advice or for help, if we need to vent, or to tell her some good news. Everything. But she is a character. People might think of her as a quiet little grandmother type, but she's not that at all. She is very blunt. She just says it how it is. She'll tell you exactly what she thinks, whether you want to hear it or not.

The Full Monte Carlo

The Girls are invited to Monte Carlo (with Hef as *their* guest) for the annual Television Festival hosted by Prince Albert. On the way they stop off in Paris for Holly and go to Saint-Tropez to celebrate Kendra's birthday. While in Monte Carlo, Kendra and Bridget go exploring and get detained by the police for making an unauthorized visit to the prince's residence.

Kendra: I loved Saint-Tropez. I loved the south of France. The south of France was my favorite place to visit. I didn't have a lot of fun in Monte Carlo because it just felt so rich and ritzy. The day that we just said "Fuck this, let's just go parasailing" is when we had a lot of fun. The rest of the time we had to be so conservative around these rich celebrities. We did that for a couple days straight and then we were like, "Let's go!"

Every Day Is Wednesday

Holly buys Hef a rare hyacinth macaw for their anniversary, in honor of the one that lived in the zoo in the seventies. Bridget takes Winnie to get an agent and she lands her first gig, as spokesdog for Hello Kitty. Kendra has a pet psychic come to the Mansion to help with Martini's issues.

Bridget: As soon as Wednesday got her first paying job, with Hello Kitty, I opened up a savings account for her. It's even titled "Wednesday." If you look at my bank statement or you go to my accounts at an ATM, it says, "Savings Account #1: Wednesday." She gets half of the money for the radio show, and her Hello Kitty money went in there, too. It's her own little fund, just in case later in life she needs something major. Maybe it's not something I can afford at the time. She has her own fund for whatever.

Go West, Young Girl

Playboy junior photo editor Holly is busy directing photo shoots, editing layouts, and testing new girls for the magazine. But she still finds time to redecorate Playboy Studio West and to take some potential Playmates out on the town with Hef, Bridget, and Kendra.

Holly: The one thing I really wanted to change were the pictures on the wall. They were all Centerfolds from the eighties, and they were really faded, old-looking pictures. Every girl on the wall was a blonde. I didn't feel like that reflected *Playboy* today. I felt like if a girl of today was coming in and thinking of posing for *Playboy* and she saw all these girls on the wall—and she's not a blonde or not white or whatever—she might look up and be like, "I don't know if this is for me." I wanted to put up some more contemporary girls and a bunch of different looks.

Jamaican Me Crazy

Holly takes Bridget and Kendra along with her to her sister's destination wedding in Jamaica. Pre-wedding activities include zip-lining, cliff diving, rehearsing for the big day, and hanging with their personal resort butler, Rory.

Bridget on cliff diving: When I got up to the forty-five-foot drop I was really nervous. This guy came crawling up the side of the cliff and told me, "Whatever you do, just step off. Don't jump out." I was like, "Really? No, I feel like I should jump out, because I can see rocks. What if I hit the edge of the cliff?" And he's like, "No, no, no, no, no. You'll lose your form and you'll do a butt flop." It took me a little bit to work up my nerve to go. When everybody out on our catamaran started counting down, I was like, "Oh, shit! Oh, shit! Now I have to do it!" In the heat of the moment, when they went "One!" I jumped out and ended up doing a butt flop, just like he said.

Wedding Belles

The wedding day arrives and maid of honor Holly spends the morning relaxing with her sister, getting massages on the beach. Meanwhile, back at the Mansion, Hef entertains some lovely ladies, while Holly tries to make contact, only to face cellular difficulties. But all is well when Holly enjoys her sister's beautiful wedding, even catching the bouquet . . . when her sister tosses it right to her.

Holly: I loved all the adventuresome things we did in Jamaica, like trying to wakeboard and zip-lining, and just spending time with my family out in the sun. That was cool. Bridget and Kendra have their families here all the time because they live in California, but I don't see my family very often. It was a nice trip. They were really excited because it was a small, intimate wedding, but since it's on the show they were able to share it with a lot more people. They were thankful for the opportunity. It was a really romantic wedding.

It's My Party and I'll Die If I Want To

Bridget throws another murder mystery birthday party, but this time she gives it a paranormal theme, with ghastly special effects. Considering that the guest list includes Barbi Benton, one wonders if there might be a real murder. But the girls are starting to bond with Hef's ex—especially Bridget and Kendra, who take a pole-dancing class with her.

Kendra on working the stripper pole: It was fun. It was not a workout at all. In any way. *It was definitely a comedy. A very, very, very funny day. That guy who gave us the lesson? Man, I don't know about him. I'd rather have a hot girl. He was not motivating me at all. I was like, "Okay." It was funny seeing Barbi. She was actually taking it seriously and I was just laughing because she was totally into it.*

Surf's Up

Bridget goes Gidget, hosting a beach party with world champion surfer Kelly Slater providing surf lessons. Kendra is pumped to meet the surfer, as she grew up riding the waves. Meanwhile, back at the Mansion, Holly takes swimming lessons from Olympic gold medalist (and *Playboy* cover girl) Amanda Beard. They all end up together again at the end of the day for a bonfire on the beach.

Bridget: I was very nervous to try surfing. I'm not afraid of swimming, and I'm not afraid of the water, but I am afraid of the ocean and I am afraid of what's in it. I worry about what's swimming around underneath me: What's coming this close to my leg? What's looking at me? I don't like that feeling. When you go somewhere where the water's crystal clear, that's different. But when you can't see, it's really scary to me. But one reason I wanted to try surfing is that I like to do things that will get me over my fears. I want to be able to do the things I want to do and not be scared.

ARC DE TRIOMPHE

Travel, Playboy Style

WORK

New York
Chicago
Las Vegas (3 work trips to Vegas)
Monte Carlo, Monaco
San Diego (2 work trips to San Diego)

PLAY

Las Vegas (3 play trips to Vegas)
Vail, Colorado
Chicago
London
Paris (2 trips to Paris)
Barcelona
Munich
Rome
Naples
Venice
Saint-Tropez

FAMILY

Fayetteville, North Carolina
Lodi, California
San Diego
Ketchikan, Alaska
Craig, Alaska
Jamaica

Around the World with The Girls Next Door

THEY'VE TRAVELED TO destinations as close as San Diego and as far as Rome. They've journeyed alone, as a trio, and with Hef and an entourage that numbered in the dozens. They've seen the sights and shows, signed memorabilia, visited family, and even dined on elk. When The Girls Next Door pack their bags, an adventure is sure to follow. ❦ **"TRAVEL IS MY** favorite thing to do," Holly declares. "First of all, traveling with Hef almost never happens because he hates to travel. He will only travel on a private plane, and when he goes anywhere, he takes a huge entourage. So it's very difficult to orchestrate a trip with Hef." But when they do, it is an event that is sure to be remembered. Whether with Hef or without, anytime the Girls leave the L.A. area, it is a massive undertaking. ❦ **SECURITY SUPERVISOR JOE** Piastro runs down the protocols involved when the Girls and Mr. Hefner go on the road: "I think we have to put the Mansion on wheels when we travel, especially with Mr. Hefner. Usually the director of security in Chicago and the West Coast manager prepare the trips. They set up all the hotel security. They'll set up ground transportation wherever we're going. Usually I get off a plane and somebody hands me the key to my hotel room so I don't have to worry about checking in. They handle any venue that Mr. Hefner and the Girls might be visiting in that particular city. ❦ **"ON MY END,** depending on where we're going, I have to handle ground transportation here in Los Angeles, along with getting the plane staff squared away, getting food on the plane, and making sure the luggage gets there. Any particular items that might be requested by Mr. Hefner or the Girls to have on the plane, it's my job to make that happen." And that's in addition to the actual job of providing the daily security. ❦ **BUT IF THE** security arrangements seem like a massive undertaking, it's nothing compared to the planning of the trip itself. "Amazing," Mary O'Connor says of the work involved in putting together the itinerary for a trip. "Amazing. It's like fly shit out of pepper. The details are just amazing. I started working on the European trip—it was in May—I started working on it in January. You have airlines, you have different

hotels, you have transportation, you have press. It's just amazing." 🐰 **ONCE THEY GET** to their destination, things get even more complicated, as Holly explains: "Anytime we travel, whether it's with Hef or without, we want to see as much as we can. And we usually only have a day or two to do it. So our schedule is packed from morning to night. It's just like *The Amazing Race*. You're running crazy all day. The itineraries are insane." In the end, it's worth it, as the Girls have enjoyed every city they've been to and the adventures that they've shared . . . in spite of having an itinerary in which one day looks something like this:

Paris

1:00 A.M. **Depart Nice**

2:45 A.M. **Arrive Paris Airport**

3:45 A.M. ARRIVE HOTEL
Four Seasons George V
31, avenue George V
75008 Paris
Tel: 33 1 49 52 70 00
Cleared for GND filming

10:00 A.M. **Depart hotel for Catacombs**

10:30 A.M. **Tour Catacombs (1 hour)**
Cleared for GND filming outside, but NOT inside

TO FOLLOW **Lunch and tour at the Louvre**
Not cleared for GND filming

7–8 P.M. **Book signing at Taschen Store (10 min. travel time)**
(GND film crew begins filming)
Press attendance expected
LOCATION
Taschen Store Paris
2, rue de Buci
75006 Paris
Tel: 33 1 40 51 79 22
Cleared for GND filming

8:30 P.M. **Dinner at L'Avenue restaurant**
ADDRESS
41, avenue Montaigne
Paris
Tel: 33 1 40 70 14 91

11:00 P.M. **Crazy Horse**
Crazy Horse is theater seating, but there's a VIP room at the back for you to enjoy cocktails,
etc., before you go to the seats.
ADDRESS
12, avenue George V
75008 Paris
Tel: 33 1 47 23 32 32
Cleared for GND filming—Hef, not GND, may even be able to get up on stage after the show

Las Vegas

(AND THE REBIRTH OF THE PLAYBOY CLUB CASINO)

It's the town that The Girls Next Door simply can't say no to. Between birthday celebrations, club openings, and appearances, Holly, Bridget, and Kendra make more trips to Sin City than to any other locale. Of course it helps that the Playboy Club and Casino has reopened at the Palms, with the Hugh Hefner Sky Villa in the Fantasy Tower as their new home away from the Mansion.

Favorite

Destinations

The Playboy Club

OCTOBER 6, 2006, was a milestone day in the Playboy Empire. It was the day that the legend was reborn . . .

The first Playboy Club opened in Chicago in 1960 and paved the way for a global enterprise, highlighted by the Playboy Club Casino in London. Hugh Hefner's trip to the opening of that London club remains, to this day, one of his most important travels. As Hef explains, "In 1966, I went to London for the opening of the Playboy Club Casino in England and I saw the future. The miniskirt had just arrived. *Time* had just done a story about the miniskirt the week before. The whole Carnaby Street/Beatles phenomenon was going on there, and everybody was there for the opening of that club—including the Beatles and everybody else. I came back to Chicago thinking about the fact that I'd been editorializing for a sexual revolution that I thought was about to occur, and I didn't want to miss it."

The Playboy Clubs expanded across the globe and prospered in the sixties and seventies. The famed Bunny waitresses became a symbol of Playboy, and being a Playboy Club key holder was, in itself, a major status symbol. But all the success took a turn in the eighties when the London operation lost its gambling license. The rest of the clubs were struggling and started to close one by one; they were gone within a few years.

Gone, but not forgotten.

In 2006, the Playboy Club Casino would reemerge at the Palms Hotel and Casino in Las Vegas, a perfect companion to the retro-cool mystique of *Playboy*. "It was a dream come true for me," Hef says of the reopening. "I had been pressing corporate in Chicago—which is run by my daughter, Christie—

PALMS
A MALOOF CASINO RESORT

WELCOME HEF & CHRISTIE HEFNER
PLAYBOY CLUB
OPENS TONIGHT
DOORS 11PM

to get us back into the Playboy Club business and the casino business. We made a deal with George Maloof at the Palms as a bellwether. It was the beginning of our move into a series of Playboy Club casinos on an international level. The next one will be a major operation in Macau, which will be open in 2009 if all goes well. And I will be doing my first visit to Asia, which, hopefully, will be on the show." Until then, the Playboy Club Casino in Las Vegas remains a popular destination for Hef and the Girls.

New York and Chicago

THE EPISODES "I'll Take Manhattan" and "My Kind of Town," when the Girls headed east to promote their first magazine pictorial, marked the first time the audience had the chance to appreciate what traveling on Playboy business is really like. The trip was a combination of work and play; Hef and the girls managed to squeeze in some sightseeing and partying between press events, magazine signings, and a rather tense appearance on *The View*.

"Going to the Statue of Liberty," Bridget responds when asked the highlight of the trip. "I've always wanted to do that. Now I've checked that off my list. It was something that I thought would be really cool and had never had an opportunity to do before." Both Holly and Kendra echo that statement, with Kendra adding, "My fondest memory was probably going to the Statue of Liberty. That was a fun time. Taking the ferry out there was a lot of fun."

It was the visit to Hef's hometown of Chicago that was the real highlight of that trip. Instead of the visit to Playboy headquarters and doing promotional events, it was the more personal sightseeing tour that really touched the Girls. "I really loved visiting the house Hef grew up in," Holly recalls. "It was funny to see him react to it, because it was much smaller than he remembered. It was cool to be able to see his home and get a peek into his childhood." Of course, while they were there, they also stopped by the original Playboy Mansion, which has now been turned into condos that Holly dreams of buying back one piece at a time.

European Tour

The trip to New York and Chicago could be seen as a warm-up to the much more involved tour of Europe Hef took the Girls on one year later in the episodes "I See London, I See France" and "When in Rome." This time the itinerary included London, Paris, Cannes, Barcelona, Munich, Rome, Naples, and Venice.

In London, Hef and the Girls toured the city, visiting the Tower of London and Hampton Court. But for Holly, a student of the French language, the highlight of the European vacation was visiting Paris and Versailles, home of Marie Antoinette.

From there they traveled south to Cannes and Barcelona, where Bridget and Kendra's plans to explore were impacted by the afternoon naps the entire city seemed to close down for. Then it was on to Bridget's native land of Germany, where she took on the role of St. Pauli girl and served beer in massive steins.

It was Italy, however, that would prove to be Bridget's weak spot. Not only was she entranced by the city of Pompeii, which she had always dreamed of visiting, but also by the place where they stayed in Venice. "The Hotel Danieli in Venice is unbelievable," Bridget says. "That was the coolest place that we've been to. Even though we'd been to Versailles, the Hotel Danieli was the one place where I really felt like I had gone back in time."

Monaco

(AND THE SOUTH OF FRANCE)

AN INVITATION FROM Prince Albert of Monaco for the Girls to attend the annual Television Festival in Monte Carlo gave them an excuse to swing by Holly's favorite spot, Paris, on the way. It also gave Kendra the chance to take a birthday trip to a place she'd always wanted to go—Saint-Tropez. "My favorite thing about Saint-Tropez was being on the beach," Kendra says. "I love the beach. I loved the drinks. I loved going out and Jet Skiing and having a great free-spirited day on the beach and taking the boat out. It was my best birthday ever."

From there, they went on to their ultimate destination, another of Holly's top sites. "I'd always wanted to visit Monaco," she says. "We got to do a lot of water sports and attend some amazing events while we were there. That is another place I love. My top three destinations are probably Paris, Disney World in Florida, and Monaco."

But not all was well in Monaco. When Bridget, Kendra, and Playmate Giuliana Marino went exploring with the cameras following, they ended up at the prince's castle and, because they were filming, wound up nearly being arrested. "Detained," Bridget quickly clarifies. "We were *detained*. I was afraid Hef was going to be pissed at us, so I stayed locked in my room the next morning. Kendra, Giuliana, and I were all sharing a room. And Kendra sleeps till whatever time, anyway. I was up, but I purposely didn't come out till Hef already knew. But he wasn't mad. He was laughing about it. His biggest concern was they confiscated our footage, and he was hoping that we would get the footage back. And then, of course, there were concerns that we hoped we didn't mess up the chances to film the rest of the events of the week, because that was right when we first got there."

But all was well, she continues. "The prince literally laughed it off. The funny thing is, we did this huge trek all the way to find his palace, and he was staying in Monte Carlo, in a place right by our hotel."

Hometown Girls

Family is clearly important to The Girls Next Door, as their parents, grandparents, brothers, sisters, and even aunts and uncles have all made visits to the show over the years. From Bridget's sister spending summers at the Mansion to Kendra's mom recuperating from surgery there to a trip to Jamaica for Holly's sister's wedding, the Girls and Hef have all become one large extended family. But nothing is more personal to each of the Girls than when they get to share their hometowns with their newest relations.

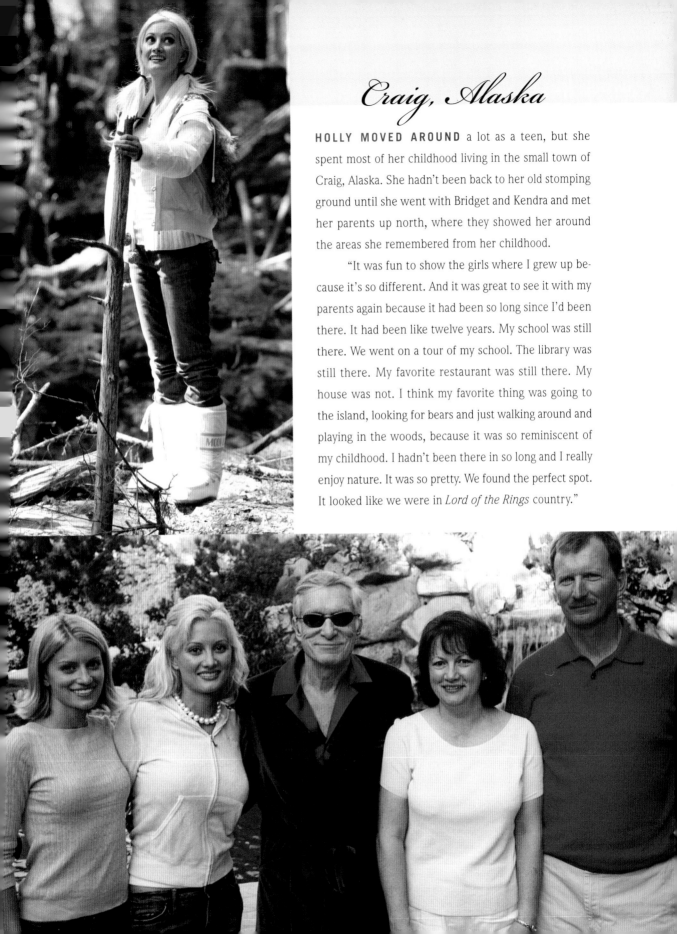

Craig, Alaska

HOLLY MOVED AROUND a lot as a teen, but she spent most of her childhood living in the small town of Craig, Alaska. She hadn't been back to her old stomping ground until she went with Bridget and Kendra and met her parents up north, where they showed her around the areas she remembered from her childhood.

"It was fun to show the girls where I grew up because it's so different. And it was great to see it with my parents again because it had been so long since I'd been there. It had been like twelve years. My school was still there. We went on a tour of my school. The library was still there. My favorite restaurant was still there. My house was not. I think my favorite thing was going to the island, looking for bears and just walking around and playing in the woods, because it was so reminiscent of my childhood. I hadn't been there in so long and I really enjoy nature. It was so pretty. We found the perfect spot. It looked like we were in *Lord of the Rings* country."

Watch Out! Alligators Please do not Touch, hit or throw things at the alligators.

Lodi, California

BRIDGET'S HOMETOWN IS slightly closer to the Mansion than Alaska, but it's still quite a trip, especially considering that when the girls visited Lodi with the production they had to do it all in one day, including the drive, which takes six hours—each way. Bridget still managed to pack a lot into the day, seeing the sights and visiting with family and friends. Now that her sister, Anastasia, lives in L.A., she does feel a bit closer to home, but it's not the same as being there.

"I don't get to go home as much as I would like to. I'm very, very, very close to my family. My parents have the luxury of being able to come here. They watch Winnie for me every time I'm going out of town. We meet halfway and they take Wednesday, because they're very much grandma and grandpa to her. But I don't see *my* grandma as much as I would like to, or my aunts and uncles. When I do go home it's very laid-back and calm. Our favorite thing to do is get some wine, stay home, barbecue, and play games. That's our fun time together."

San Diego, California

THEY SAY GETTING there is half the fun, and Kendra had a blast taking the Playboy private railcar down to San Diego so Hef and the Girls could see her home. "There was a lot you didn't see, too," she says with a mischievous grin. "I flashed a lot of people." But her breasts weren't the only sights the group saw, as they visited with her mom and took a private bus around town.

"I just love being in my city and being around San Diego fans. I love the feeling of being there. I grew up loving the Chargers and everything. My favorite part was when Hef was loving watching my video of me as a kid. I love that he came to San Diego. It was the craziest feeling ever. But when he was watching my home videos, that part was my favorite. It showed me that he really cared to know where I'd come from and who I was back then."

To Live and Dine in L.A.

WHY TRAVEL WHEN you live in one of the most exciting places in the world? Here are just a few of the many things the Girls like to do when they're exploring the city that they now call home.

THE PLAYBOY JAZZ FESTIVAL AT THE HOLLYWOOD BOWL

2301 North Highland Ave., Hollywood
www.hollywoodbowl.com

Traditionally held on Father's Day weekend, The Playboy Jazz Festival originated in 1959 at Chicago Stadium. But it was the second festival, held twenty years later, that became an annual event when it found a home at the Hollywood Bowl. The festival is one of the highlights of the year for the Mansion residents. "They have all kinds of **ECLECTIC JAZZ ACTS** every year," Holly explains. "It's a two-day festival. We usually go on Saturday. We pack these awesome picnic baskets and we go and spend the whole day outside. We usually invite some friends. Most of Hef's family goes, like Christie and David and Keith. It's a great day with a lot of friends and family."

CULVER ICE ARENA
4545 Sepulveda Blvd., Culver City
www.culvericearena.com

"Before we started taping the show," Bridget recalls, "I did a Winter Wonderland party for Holly's birth-day and we went to an ice-skating rink." The party served as the inspiration for the girls day out in "New Girls in Town," even though Bridget freely admits that **ICE-SKATING** isn't exactly her cup of tea. "I enjoy it. I'm not good at it, but I do enjoy it. At least I can let go of the sides, unlike other people [giggles]."

LUCKY STRIKE LANES
6801 Hollywood Blvd., Suite 143, Hollywood (and over a dozen other locations)
www.bowlluckystrike.com

Hef took the Girls out to **BOWL** a few sets in "Grape Expectations." While they all had a good time, the show failed to capture one important element of the evening: "I won!" Kendra proudly proclaims. "But they didn't show that. They showed the one time I put it in the gutter and then they replayed it over and over again so it looked like I kept throwing gutter balls. But I won!"

THE HOLLYWOOD IMPROV
8162 Melrose Ave., Hollywood
www.improv.com

The Hollywood Improv is the second in a chain of popular **COMEDY** clubs that have showcased some of the most talented comedians in the country, including February 1986 Playmate and actress Julie McCul-lough, as seen in "We Can Work It Out."

SUNSET RANCH
3400 N. Beachwood Dr., Hollywood
www.sunsetranchhollywood.com

Tucked into the Hollywood Hills, Sunset Ranch offers **HORSEBACK RIDES** through Griffith Park, along with a meal at the Viva Fresh Mexican Restaurant. (Though, as the Girls learned in "May the Horse Be with You," it is not advisable to drink and ride.) "That was fun," Bridget recalls. "I loved it. I hadn't been horseback riding since I was young and lived back in Galt and Lodi."

RANCHO PARK COURSE
10460 Pico Blvd., Los Angeles
www.golf.lacity.org

When she's not in the mood to hit the batting cage, Kendra takes her friends to the driving range at this public **GOLF** course in Los Angeles, like she did with Monica Leigh in "PMOY Not?"

THE ORPHEUM THEATRE

842 S. Broadway, Los Angeles

www.laorpheum.com

Film buff Hugh Hefner sponsored a screening of *Flesh and the Devil* at this landmark L.A. classic movie theater in "Training Daze." Hef's love of film is something that has been with him since his childhood. "At a very early age, I escaped into the dreams and fantasies that were fueled by and large by the movies of the thirties and early forties." He credits these films, and Betty Grable in particular, as being his inspiration for the original girl next door.

RENAISSANCE PLEASURE FAIRE

15501 E. Arrow Hwy., Irwindale

www.renfair.com/socal

This is an event that Bridget attends every year; last year she managed to convince Hef and the Girls to join her in "Surely, You Joust." Bridget grew up working at her local Renaissance Faire and fully embraces the atmosphere. "The faire lifestyle is crazy!" she enthuses. "It's a great time for people to dress up and become completely immersed in a whole different era, culture, and lifestyle, if just for the day. You can be whoever you want to be, from peasant to royalty."

CRUNCH GYM

8000 Sunset Blvd., Los Angeles (and other locations throughout L.A.)

www.crunch.com

More than just a place for lifting weights, Crunch Gym offers classes in all the latest **WORKOUT TRENDS**, including the proper way to work a stripper pole (as seen in "It's My Party and I'll Die If I Want To"). Celeb sightings are frequent at this popular fitness club, and you never know who you might see working out.

DISNEYLAND

Anaheim

www.disneyland.com

Though it's never been seen on the show because the production company cannot get the clearance to film there, Disneyland—and Disney's worldwide theme parks—play an integral part in **HOLLY'S** life. As she explains, "I always say *The Girls Next Door* will never capture my complete life because they can't follow me to Disneyland."

GEISHA HOUSE

6633 Hollywood Blvd., Hollywood

www.dolcegroup.com/geisha

This spot is popular with the show, as Hef and the Girls have visited on more than one occasion (though the kitchen does move faster when it doesn't have cameras getting in the way). Holly recommends the **MARILYN MONROLL** and the Hollywood Roll.

KATANA

8439 W. Sunset Blvd., West Hollywood

www.katanarobata.com/katana

This Japanese restaurant is, by far, the favorite place to dine for all the Mansion denizens. Bridget speaks for all the Girls when she calls this her "favorite restaurant. Forget the ambiance. Forget everything else. I love their food. It's so delicious, and it's pretty **HEALTHY**. I just absolutely love it there." Kendra, who doesn't eat seafood, highly recommends the chicken teriyaki.

MASTRO'S STEAKHOUSE

246 N. Canon Dr., Beverly Hills

www.mastrossteakhouse.com

This restaurant is another favorite of the girls; Kendra celebrated her twenty-first birthday here with Hef and her family in "The 21 Club." Kendra says: "I don't eat steak unless it's Mastro's. I don't eat any other steak—period. Mastro's steak is the **BEST STEAK**. It's worth it."

TRADER VIC'S

www.tradervics.com

Though the Beverly Hills location seen in "Hearts Afire" is now closed, this restaurant still boasts more than two dozen locations worldwide and remains a favorite of Holly's. She says: "I had three **FAVORITE DRINKS** there, and I would get so drunk because every time I went I had to get each one: the Pink Cloud, the Peachtree Punch, and the Blue Hawaiian. And then we always had to get a Scorpion Bowl, too, just because it's the Scorpion Bowl."

THE MELTING POT

www.meltingpot.com

Although this is one of Holly's favorite restaurants, the production could not film there for the show. That didn't stop the Mansion staff from visiting the **FONDUE** restaurant and taking copious notes so they could re-create the menu for "Hef's Melting Pot" on Hef and Holly's fifth anniversary, celebrated in "The Age of Aquarium." Holly recommends starting with the cheese course (her favorite is the artichoke), followed by a California salad with raspberry dressing. For the chocolate course her favorite is the Yin/Yang, a white and dark chocolate fondue designed to resemble the yin and yang symbol.

RED LION TAVERN
2366 Glendale Blvd., Los Angeles
www.redliontavern.net

This is a place Bridget can go to celebrate her **GERMAN** heritage, as she did with Playmate of the Year candidate Janine Habeck in "PMOY Not?" Self-described picky eater Bridget recommends the Wiener schnitzel. "I thought it was going to be like a hot dog or a sausage or something. It was a pounded-out piece of meat, breaded and fried. . . . Oh, my gosh, everything was so good there, I was dying."

SADDLE RANCH CHOP HOUSE

8371 Sunset Blvd., Los Angeles

www.srrestaurants.com

This is the fun Western-themed restaurant where Hef and the Girls took some potential Playmate candidates in "Go West, Young Girl." Holly recommends riding the mechanical bull.

MEL'S DRIVE IN

8585 Sunset Blvd., West Hollywood

www.melsdrive-in.com

This California diner chain is a fun place to kick back **FIFTIES-STYLE**, as seen in "Midsummer Night's Dream." Holly recommends "the burgers, of course."

DAVE & BUSTER'S

www.daveandbusters.com

This chain of restaurants/entertainment arcades, seen in "Family Affairs," is very important to *The Girls Next Door* history, as **KENDRA** was at the San Diego location with her family when Hef called to ask her to move in to the Mansion.

HOOTERS

www.hooters.com

Though this restaurant has dozens and dozens of locations across the country, Holly still feels a kinship with the L.A. branch of the restaurant, at which she worked when she moved to the city. **HOLLY** took her fellow Hooters workers and Playmate of the Year candidates Sara Underwood and Alison Waite there in "PMOY Not?" and she often stops by the restaurants in search of potential Playmates. Holly recommends just about everything on the menu.

SPRINKLES CUPCAKES

9635 Little Santa Monica Blvd., Beverly Hills

www.sprinklescupcakes.com

Bridget is so in love with this little cupcake bakery that she's become friends with the owner and calls him up personally when she's in the mood for a Sprinkles fix. **BRIDGET** recommends the "vanilla. By far, vanilla's my favorite."

OLIVE GARDEN

www.olivegarden.com

Kendra is a **HUGE FAN** of this Italian restaurant chain. Though it hasn't been seen on the show, the Olive Garden has been mentioned on numerous occasions, and a gift certificate to the restaurant makes the perfect present for her. Kendra recommends the "Tour of Italy," a meal that combines lasagna, chicken parmigiana, and fettuccine Alfredo, all on one plate.

The Mansion Menagerie

Holly's Furry Friends

Harlow: POMERANIAN
Panda: POMERANIAN
Duchess: CHIHUAHUA
Duke: CHIHUAHUA

THE PUPPY PARADE marching through the Mansion is full of exuberant energy, especially when the cameras are around. Each of Holly's pups has its own distinct personality, whether Mom likes it or not. Harlow is the demanding diva who likes to have things her way. Panda is the black-and-white bandit who makes a dash for the outdoor kitchen to pilfer food any time she is let out. Duchess is the recovering "rescue" who is becoming more social every day and makes friends wherever she goes. And Duke, fittingly, is the playboy of the bunch, who particularly loves to play with Bridget's baby, Winnie. The two can often be found chasing each other, and they even shared a romantic golf-cart ride on Valentine's Day.

While Holly's away, her pets may play, but the Mansion staff has additional duties, related to doo-die. Whenever Holly takes extended trips from the Mansion, this is the list of instructions she leaves behind for the proper care and maintenance of her little darlings and her pet birds:

INSTRUCTIONS RE: HOLLY'S PETS

1. Please **TAKE THE DOGS OUTSIDE** at least 3 times a day. I usually do it at 9am, 3pm, and 9pm.

2. Please **FEED THE DOGS** Natural Balance wet food in the morning and dry food at 4 or 5 pm. Please give Harlow a dash of Flex with each serving of food.

3. Please **COVER THE BIRDS' CAGE** at 9 or 10 pm, and uncover them in the morning.

4. Please make sure the birds have **FRESH SEED EVERY DAY**. I will leave a large bag of it on the desk in the bathroom. Also, make sure their water has not run out.

5. Please **CHANGE THE PAPER-TOWEL LINER** in the birdcage once a day.

Thank you!
Love,
Holly

Bridget's Babies

Wednesday "Winnie" Addams: PEKINGESE

Gizmo "Gizzie": PERSIAN

THE CAMERAS FOLLOWED Bridget as she picked up little Wednesday Addams during the brief stopover in Atlanta on her flight back from visiting her brother in North Carolina. Unlike her mother, Wednesday doesn't seem to be into costumes and will go flat-out "dogatonic" if Bridget even tries to dress her up. But when it comes to her career, Wednesday is always a professional, though Bridget isn't the typical stage mom. "I'm not pushing her to do much," Bridget says. "I'm very, very picky. It's only really good jobs. She doesn't need to work, so it's only a matter of if it's something super cool I think she'd be perfect for." Bridget rewards Winnie's work efforts. Winnie's favorite treats are Pup-Peroni, bell peppers, and roasted chicken.

The lone cat in the Girls' personal menagerie, Gizmo is definitely the independent one in the group. "She only wants loving when she wants loving," Bridget explains. "And the rest of the time, it's 'Screw you. Don't mess with me.' But she's very, very lovable. Sometimes people come in my room and she just runs up to them and starts rubbing on them. But then my sister will come over, 'cause she's here quite a bit, and will go to grab her, and she's like 'Roooowrr! Don't pick me up.'" Gizzie has staked her claim on several spots in Bridget's bedroom as her favorites, and can often be found curled up in the sink, in the bathtub, or at the back of Bridget's closet. She also likes to lie in the sun on the bench seat of the dormer window. But her tree is the number one favorite spot for her to get away from it all.

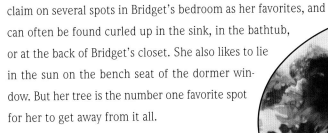

Kendra's Kritters

Raskal: WELSH CORGI

Martini: JACK RUSSELL TERRIER

LIKE A REASONABLY priced sparkling wine, Martini and Raskal are as bubbly as their mother. "They both have my personality," Kendra proudly exclaims. "They both have it, but different sides of it, because I'm a Gemini. Raskal's like a total momma's boy. He has a shy side. He's very shy, and very much a homebody. He wants to be home and relax with me. Martini is the tomboy. She goes out and plays ball. She's the social butterfly of the house. They both reflect me so much."

Though he may be on the shy side, Raskal does get excited when his momma is around and will gleefully join her in her afternoon workout, providing a little extra weight for her while she does her push-ups by jumping on her back.

But all is not perfect with Kendra's pooches. As seen in the episode "Every Day Is Wednesday," Martini has an OCD affliction where she sees light and starts chasing it. This is more common in Jack Russell Terriers than in most dogs, being an outgrowth of their hunting instinct, although Kendra tried an uncommon cure. "I didn't really want a dog psychic," Kendra says. "I wanted a fuckin' dog therapist, because Martini, she seriously has a problem right now. She really does. It's really bad." But in spite of those issues, Kendra has a deep love for her babies, as do all of The Girls Next Door.

IN LOVING MEMORY

Little Foot
1994–2007

Archie
1995–2008

The Mansion Zoo

THE PLAYBOY MANSION is home to more than one hundred species of birds, as well as monkeys, reptiles, amphibians, tropical fish, and, of course, bunnies. The animal department is charged with the care and feeding of these zoo residents, which include three pairs of birds on the endangered species list that make a different kind of mating a particularly important activity at the Playboy Mansion. 🐰 **ONE OF THE** most famous of the zoo residents is Coco the spider monkey. Holly has the closest bond with Coco and brings her out to play during the Fun in the Sun Sundays and makes sure she gets her much-needed exercise. "Coco's doing awesome!" Holly enthuses. "We're walking her a lot and she's spending a lot of time outside of her cage, so she's doing really well and making a lot of new friends. I just love seeing her interact with people. I also love bringing her out back by the tennis courts because we have a little orange grove back there where I can take her to pick oranges." 🐰 **THOUGH ALL THE** Mansion residents and staff have a fondness for the many animals on the property, Holly in particular has taken an active interest in the Mansion zoo. She works with the staff to stock the zoo with Hef's favorite animals, often relying on this to provide her with gift inspiration when shopping for the man who has everything . . . including her. 🐰 **HOLLY IS OFTEN** seen around the Mansion with Lady Macbeth, one of the most recent acquisitions, on her arm. The rare hyacinth macaw was obtained in honor of the original Macbeth that Hef had in the zoo in the seventies. "She's so sweet," Holly says. "She's doing really well. Although she does like to test her boundaries a lot and try to bite me. I have to be careful with my jewelry and my zippers and things. She always tries to eat them." 🐰 **IT ISN'T UNUSUAL** to see the animals roaming the premises, as the zoo was conceived under the philosophy of minimum confinement. Mansion guests are instructed to take care when driving onto the grounds, as one never knows when a stray peacock may be crossing the path.

THE CONCEPT OF the private kitchen that operates around the clock originated with the Chicago Playboy Mansion. Once upon a time, Hugh Hefner spent a lot of time traveling and often stayed at hotels where the kitchens closed at midnight. This left little option for a late-night snack. When he developed the lifestyle that accompanied his new home, Hef determined that one of the main components of achieving the level of personal comfort he desired would be to install what has become known as the 24-Hour Kitchen.

MORE THAN SIMPLY a cook that can be rung up any hour of the day or night, the kitchen of the current Playboy Mansion is a full-service operation. Under the supervision of executive chef William S. Bloxsom-Carter, the kitchen creates the menus for all manner of event, from the weekend buffets to corporate events to Hef's personal parties with guest lists that number a thousand or more. 🐰 **THE STAFF OF** approximately twenty chefs is augmented by an internship program in which culinary students from all over the country have the opportunity to learn in a practical setting. The program is responsible for bringing pastry chef Laurie Rodgers to the Mansion, who left her job as an office manager after twenty-five years and decided to give culinary school a try. "It's something I never thought would happen," Laurie explains. "I went to culinary school and did my internship at the Playboy Mansion, and I was fortunate in that a position became available and I was hired on. So this is actually my only professional pastry-chef job. I've never worked anywhere else." 🐰 **BEYOND PROVIDING FOOD** for the parties, the 24-Hour Kitchen is, first and foremost, the place where Hef and The Girls Next Door can go when they're hungry. Whether they're in the mood for a quick bite or a full meal, whatever taste they desire is only a call away. "We have a checklist of inventory," Laurie explains. "We have one for Mr. Hefner. We have one for just the house general items. And we have a Girls' Checklist. We pretty much know what they like. Occasionally there's something that we don't have and they'll just ask, 'Oh, can you get it?' And we get it for them. We don't keep things like lobster tails on hand, but for the most part, we've got what they want." 🐰 **WHEN THE GIRLS** find something they like at a restaurant, they can bring it back to the kitchen staff to re-create and add to the inventory. And each of the Girls has also brought her own personal tastes to the kitchen. Holly's mom's recipe for flaky warm rolls is now served regularly at the weekend buffets, and Bridget's family recipe for cottage cheese dip is a staple at snack time. 🐰 **IN THE FOLLOWING** pages, the Girls and the Mansion chefs have opened up their personal recipe files to share with the show's fans.

Holly's Favorite Recipes

HOLLY'S MOM'S GREEK SALAD

2 packages Near East roasted garlic and olive oil flavor couscous

1 can small whole black olives, drained

1 bunch green onions, chopped

1 diced green pepper

1 diced bunch radishes

1 large cucumber, diced

6 oz. crumbled feta cheese

Prepare couscous and allow to cool. Mix in other ingredients. Chill.

HOLLY'S MOM'S PASTA SALAD: CONFETTI SPAGHETTI

16 oz. spaghetti, cooked

16 oz. Bernstein's Italian Dressing (such as cheese and garlic)

1 cubed cucumber

1 large grated carrot

1 bunch sliced green onions

1 diced green pepper

1 cup cubed sharp cheddar

1 cup cubed Monterey Jack cheese

$^1/_2$ cup shredded red cabbage (add just before serving because it stains the noodles)

Combine all ingredients. Marinate in dressing for a couple of hours. (An extra bottle of dressing can come in handy, as the other ingredients tend to soak it all up.)

HOLLY'S MOM'S ROLL RECIPE
(SERVED REGULARLY AT THE MANSION BUFFET)

$1^1/_4$ cups milk, warmed

$^1/_3$ cup sugar

2 tsp. salt

1 package yeast

4 tbsp. butter, softened

1 egg

$3^1/_2$ to $4^1/_2$ cups flour

Stir the warm milk, sugar, and salt together in large mixing bowl. ❀ Sprinkle on the yeast. Stir and let dissolve. Add butter, egg, and two cups flour. Beat vigorously. Add more flour, enough to make a manageable dough. Turn out onto a lightly floured surface and knead 6–8 minutes, until smooth and elastic. Place in large greased bowl and cover with plastic. Let rise in warm spot till doubled. Divide in two balls. Roll out to a 12-inch circle. ❀ Brush with $^1/_4$ cup melted butter. Cut into 12 wedges. Roll each wedge from wide edge in and place on greased cookie sheet. Cover with plastic and let rise until double. Bake in preheated oven at 375 degrees for 12–15 minutes.

HOLLY'S MOM'S CHOCOLATE CHIP COOKIE RECIPE

1 cup butter, softened

2 cups brown sugar

2 eggs

2 tsp. vanilla

$^1/_2$ tsp. baking soda

1 tsp. baking powder

$^1/_4$ tsp. salt

2 cups flour

2 cups oatmeal

1 package chocolate chips

Cream butter and brown sugar. Add eggs, vanilla, baking soda, baking powder, and salt. Stir in flour and oatmeal, then chocolate chips. Drop by spoonfuls onto greased cookie sheet. ❀ Bake at 350 degrees for about 11 minutes.

Bridget's Favorite Recipes

THE CASE FAMILY COTTAGE CHEESE DIP

16 oz. low-fat, small-curd cottage cheese

8 oz. package of low-fat cream cheese

3/4 cup of non-fat mayo

Red wine vinegar, to taste . . . I like a lot!!

Celery salt

Pepper

Blend ingredients together. ❊ This dish is best if refrigerated for a few hours before serving.
Serve with reduced-fat Ruffles or vegetables (sliced carrots, cherry tomatoes, cucumbers, bell
peppers).

BRIDGET'S SPECIAL GUACAMOLE

3 large avocados

1 tomato, diced

$^1/_2$ small red onion, diced

salt and pepper, to taste

Mash the avocados and add the remaining ingredients.

BRIDGET'S FAMOUS BEAN DIP

1 can refried beans

$^1/_4$ cup water

3 tbsp. Taco Bell Seasoning Mix

1 cup shredded cheddar

3–4 flour tortillas

Blend beans in food processor until smooth. ❋ Place beans, water, and seasoning mix in frying pan and cook until heated through. Place half of the beans in a bowl, cover with half of the cheddar, layer with more beans, and top with remaining cheddar. Place in broiler until cheese melts. Serve with warm flour tortillas.

PITA PIZZA (HEALTHY PIZZAS FOR PEOPLE AND DOGS)

1 whole pita bread

$^1/_2$ cup Prego tomato sauce

$^1/_4$ cup sliced black olives

$^1/_4$ cup diced tomatoes

$^1/_4$ cup diced pepperoncini

$^1/_2$ cup shredded mozzarella

Warm pita in broiler, then place on cast-iron skillet. Top with sauce, black olives, diced tomatoes, pepperoncini, and mozzarella. Place in preheated 350-degree oven until heated throughout and cheese is melted. ❋ **NOTE** For dogs, use a whole-wheat pita, cheese, sauce, bell peppers, and vegetarian pepperoni.

MANSION WOK-CHARRED GREEN BEANS AND BEEF

$^1/_2$ lb. filet mignon, cut into cubes and seasoned with salt and pepper

$^1/_2$ cup green beans, steamed

1 tbsp. Chinese chili garlic sauce

1 tbsp. hoisin sauce

1 tbsp. black bean and garlic paste

3 tbsp. soy sauce

Heat wok with a small amount of cooking oil. Sear beef, add green beans, garlic sauce, hoisin sauce, black bean and garlic paste, and soy sauce. Heat through and serve immediately.

MANSION CHICKEN TACOS

1 tbsp. vegetable oil

Taco Bell Seasoning Mix

2 chicken breasts, cubed, seasoned with salt and pepper

2 flour tortillas

Lettuce

Tomatoes

Cheese

Combine oil, taco seasoning mix, and cubed chicken in a bowl and coat thoroughly. Grill in cast-iron skillet or wok until blackened. Place chicken in warmed tortilla. Add shredded lettuce, diced tomatoes, and grated cheese.

MANSION SPICY TUNA ROLLS

4–6 oz. fresh raw tuna

1 tbsp. low-fat mayonnaise

1 tsp. Chinese hot sauce

Sushi rice

Blend tuna, mayonnaise, and hot sauce in food processor. ◉ Cook sushi rice, place on sheet pan to cool, then form rice into 2-inch squares, and grill on both sides. ◉ Put tuna mixture on top and serve immediately.

Kendra's Favorite Recipes

SANDY EGGO

> 1 Eggo waffle
>
> Butter
>
> 1 tbsp. sugar
>
> 1 tbsp. cinnamon
>
> 1 Ziploc bag
>
> Maple syrup (optional)

Prepare waffle as directed on package. Lightly butter waffle. Pour sugar and cinnamon into Ziploc bag. Place waffle in bag. Shake. Remove. ❀ Top with maple syrup if desired.

CAPTAIN BOB'S GRILLED HAM AND CHEESE SANDWICH

Butter

2 slices white Wonder Bread

2 slices American cheese

1 slice ham

1 snack and sandwich maker

Butter the outside of each piece of bread. Place a slice of cheese on the dry side of the bottom piece of bread. Add slice of ham. Add second slice of cheese. Top with second slice of bread. Heat in sandwich maker. (Time may vary depending on sandwich maker.)

MANSION CHINESE CHICKEN SALAD

2 chicken breasts, baked and shredded

1 head iceberg lettuce, chopped

1 bunch green onions, chopped finely

1 can chow mein noodles

2 tbsp. sliced or slivered almonds

2 tbsp. sesame seeds

Girard's Chinese Chicken Salad Dressing

Combine all ingredients except dressing. Toss gently. Top with salad dressing.

MANSION FRIED CHICKEN

2 chicken breasts, split

2 chicken thighs

6 chicken drumsticks

1$\frac{1}{2}$ cups Wesson oil

SEASONED FLOUR

3 cups all-purpose flour

1$\frac{1}{2}$ tbsp. Lawry's Seasoned Salt

$\frac{1}{2}$ tsp. ground black pepper

$\frac{1}{2}$ tsp. fine sea salt

1 tbsp. Spanish paprika

Preheat an electric skillet to 375 degrees. Rinse the chicken pieces thoroughly in cold running water. Pour in the Wesson oil. Let the oil heat up. Test by sprinkling some flour in the pan. If it bubbles, the oil is hot enough to start frying the chicken. ❋ Fully dredge the wet chicken in the flour mixture and place in the skillet. Reserve the seasoned flour. Cover and allow to steam/fry for 15 minutes. Remove the cover and sprinkle a small amount of seasoned flour over the top of all the chicken pieces. Chicken should be a nice golden brown before turning (approximately 25 minutes). Brown the other side (approximately 15–20 minutes). Remove the chicken pieces from the skillet. Place on paper towels to drain. Set aside and keep warm. Turn off the skillet. ❋ Using a strainer, pour off all the oil, reserving 2 tablespoons to make the gravy. A strainer must be used for this procedure. It is important to reserve all the fried crispies from the skillet oil.

GRAVY

1 can Campbell's Cream of Chicken Soup

$1/2$ cup regular milk

$1/2$ tbsp. strained fry oil (from frying the chicken)

2 tbsp. seasoned flour

Combine the Campbell's Cream of Chicken soup with the milk. Heat over medium high flame, stirring frequently to avoid burning. When heated thoroughly, remove from the heat and keep warm. ❋ Reheat the electric skillet to 350 degrees. Add the reserved fry oil and crispies to the skillet. Add the seasoned flour and combine to form a roux. Brown lightly for approximately 7 minutes. Add the warmed soup/milk mixture stirring well to incorporate. When the mixture begins to thicken, turn the skillet temperature down to 200 degrees. Add more milk to get a proper gravy consistency and then turn off the skillet. When reheating the gravy to serve with the meal, add more milk to achieve desired consistency.

HUGH HEFNER'S LAMB CHOP DINNER

LAMB CHOPS

4 fresh French-cut lamb chops (from 3-pound rack—see note*)

1 tbsp. seasoning salt

1 tsp. ground white pepper

$^{1}/_{2}$ tsp. olive oil

LAMB SAUCE

1 can Campbell's beef broth

$^{1}/_{2}$ cup cold water

$1^{1}/_{2}$ tsp. Swiss Chalet Pro Thick vegetable starch thickener
($^{1}/_{4}$ tsp. of cornstarch mixed with $^{1}/_{4}$ tsp. water can be substituted)

1 sprig fresh rosemary, 4 inches long

(*NOTE Order from the butcher: a French-cut prime lamb rack weighing about three pounds.)

PREPARING THE LAMB CHOPS

Trim lamb chops of all excess fat. Trim should include the bone to the eye of the chop. Season the chops with salt and ground white pepper. Place the olive oil on a plate; dip the chops in the olive oil. In a very hot, preheated sauté pan, sear the chops on both sides until they are dark brown, three minutes per side. Cover pan and let chops sit on a low flame for an additional two minutes.

✻ The fourth chop is for the cook to eat and determine if it is tender and tasty. If it is acceptable, serve the remaining three to Mr. Hefner. If it is not tender or tasty, start the process again by cutting from another rack of lamb.

PREPARING THE SAUCE

Combine the beef broth and water. Bring to a simmer. Whisk in the Pro Thick and return to a simmer. Add the rosemary sprig and cook for 20–30 seconds. Remove the rosemary sprig from the sauce. Keep the sauce warm.

PREPARING THE BAKED POTATO

Wash three 90-count-size potatoes. Wrap in foil and bake in oven at 350 degrees for 90 minutes or until done. Remove from oven and place in warmer until dinner is requested. Choose the best potato; remove foil and place on plate.

PREPARING PEAS

Open one can of Le Sueur Early Peas (15 oz.) and heat in skillet. Season lightly with a pinch of fine sea salt and 1 tsp. salted butter when heating. Serve about one-third of the peas in a side bowl when the dinner is served.

PREPARING TOMATO

Cut from the center of a beefsteak tomato (4-inch x 5-inch) two slices of tomato ½-inch thick. Place the slices on a small side plate that has been lined with the top half of a washed leaf of romaine lettuce.

PLATE PRESENTATION

Place the three lamb chops on a warm HMH dinner plate. The bones should be pointing to the center of the plate. Spoon a little of the sauce over each chop and allow some to flow slightly onto the plate around each chop. Place the baked potato next to the chops, with no sauce touching it. No butter is put into the potato. Real butter (not margarine or butter substitute) and salt should be served on the side. The peas and applesauce are placed in small bowls on the side.

WHEN SERVING

When Mr. Hefner calls for his dinner everything should be ready before cooking the chops. When the chops are completed, a butler should serve the meal immediately.

Trivia Quiz

1. Complete this song lyric from *The Girls Next Door* theme: *I'm gonna give you figs, and dates, and grapes, and . . .*

   a. kumquats   b. crepes   c. cakes   d. the flu

2. In the opening animation, what letter is Holly wearing on her cheerleader uniform?

   a. H   b. M   c. P   d. Q

3. In the opening animation during the first season, what item is *not* in Bridget's room?

   a. ball of yarn   b. jack-o'-lantern   c. Gizzie   d. Winnie

4. In the opening animation, Kendra is wearing a jersey for which sports team?

   a. Eagles   b. Chargers   c. Angels   d. Lakers

5. In the opening animation, in what order are the Girls and Hef standing during their bobble-head pose (from left to right)?

   a. Kendra, Bridget, Hef, Holly   b. Bridget, Kendra, Hef, Holly

   c. Holly, Hef, Kendra, Bridget   d. Hef, Holly, Bridget, Kendra

6. Where was **HOLLY** born?

    a. Alaska   b. Oregon   c. California   d. Disneyland

7. Which of the following is *not* the name of one of Holly's dogs?

    a. Duchess   b. Panda   c. Hepburn   d. Harlow

8. What Disney character did Holly dress up as to attend the Renaissance Faire in "Surely, You Joust"?

    a. Snow White.   b. Sleeping Beauty.   c. Cinderella.   d. Jasmine.

9. What is a "puffin"?

    a. a brand of marshmallow   b. a seabird that looks like a penguin
    c. a magic dragon   d. a playboy known to smoke a pipe

10. What did Holly give Hef for their fifth anniversary?

    a. a hyacinth macaw   b. a pair of white peacocks   c. tropical fish   d. a striptease

11. What circus-related activity does **BRIDGET** study?

    a. lion taming   b. clowning   c. tightrope walking   d. trapeze

12. What breed of dog is Wednesday?

    a. Pekingese   b. poodle   c. Pomeranian   d. German shepherd

13. On what day does Bridget and Wednesday's talk show air?

    a. Monday   b. Tuesday   c. Thursday   d. Friday

14. Who built the cake that Bridget popped out of on Hef's eightieth birthday?

    a. Bridget   b. Hank   c. Captain Bob   d. Gizmo

15. Which of Bridget's family members came to the Mansion to help with Coco the spider monkey's diet?

    a. Anastasia   b. Aunt Vicky   c. Aunt Jane   d. her mother

16. What is **KENDRA**'s favorite restaurant?

    a. Spago   b. Geisha House   c. Olive Garden   d. Red Lobster

17. Who gives Kendra a pimp cup on her twenty-first birthday?

    a. TV Johnny   b. Don "Magic" Juan   c. Captain Bob   d. Hef

18. Which vehicle is Kendra most afraid of traveling in?

    a. race car   b. train   c. airplane   d. speedboat

19. When Kendra bought a G-string for Carmella DeCesare as an emergency gift, what was written on the underwear?

    a. "Playmate of the Year"   b. "Just Married"   c. "Ride the Bride"   d. "Bride-thrilla"

20. When shooting the 2008 calendar, what classic movie star does Kendra liken herself to?

    a. Jean Harlow   b. Mae West   c. Ginger Rogers   d. Betty Grable

21. What is **HUGH HEFNER**'s preferred drink?
    a. Jack Daniel's   b. tequila   c. scotch and soda   d. Sex on the Beach

22. Where is Hef's famed rotating bed from the original Playboy Mansion now located?
    a. Hef and Holly's bedroom   b. the guesthouse   c. the gamehouse   d. the Playmate house

23. Which of Hef's children is CEO of Playboy Enterprises?
    a. Christie   b. David   c. Marston   d. Cooper

24. What is Hef's favorite board game?
    a. chess   b. Chinese checkers   c. backgammon   d. Mouse Trap

25. Who did Hef portray when he went to the Renaissance Faire in "Surely, You Joust"?
    a. the King of France   b. the King of Spain   c. the King of England   d. Elvis

26. When did Hugh Hefner purchase the Playboy Mansion West?
    a. 1953   b. 1965   c. 1971   d. 1985

27. Which of the Mansion parties shares its name with a Shakespeare play?
    a. Tempest   b. As You Like It   c. Midsummer Night's Dream   d. All's Well That Ends Well

28. In what part of Los Angeles is the Mansion located?
    a. Brentwood   b. Holmby Hills   c. Bel Air   d. Inglewood

29. What is the name of the series of regular Sunday afternoon parties during the warm-weather months?
    a. Sunny Bunnies   b. Grotto Games   c. Hef's Pool Party   d. Fun in the Sun

30. Who is rumored to haunt the Mansion?
    a. Mrs. Letts   b. Mrs. Davies   c. Casper   d. Barbi Benton

ANSWERS

1=c · 2=c · 3=d · 4=b · 5=a · 6=b · 7=c · 8=b · 9=b (and maybe d) · 10=c · 11=d · 12=a · 13=d · 14=c · 15=c · 16=c · 17=b · 18=c · 19=c · 20=b · 21=a · 22=d · 23=a · 24=c · 25=a · 26=c · 27=c · 28=b · 29=d · 30=a

ACKNOWLEDGMENTS

First and foremost, a tremendous amount of thanks and appreciation go out to Holly Madison, Bridget Marquardt, and Kendra Wilkinson for giving up hours on end to discuss this book, for the many e-mails back and forth, and for all the writing you contributed. Additional thanks go out to everyone at Playboy and the Mansion for making me feel like part of the family, especially Carlena Bryant, Chef William S. Bloxsom-Carter, Anastasia Case, Bob Colin, Jon (J.D.) Davis, Hank Fawcett, Leopold Froehlich, Rob Hilburger, Elizabeth Kanski, Bonnie Jean Kenny, Bradley Lincoln, Elayne Lodge, Alan Loeb, Steve Martinez, Norma Meister, Joyce Nizzari, Mary O'Connor (and Captain Bob), Brian Olea, Joe Piastro, Laurie Rodgers, Dick Rosenzweig, and Amanda Warren. And to all the folks at Prometheus Entertainment, particularly Kevin Burns, Scott Hartford, Amy Prenner, and Mykelle Sabin. And to everyone at Simon Spotlight Entertainment, especially Jennifer Heddle, Jaime Cerota, Jennifer Bergstrom, and Anthony Ziccardi.

And, finally, special thanks and heartfelt gratitude to Mr. Hugh M. Hefner.

The following resource was invaluable for providing insight into this project:
Inside the Playboy Mansion by Gretchen Edgren © 1998 by Playboy Enterprises, Inc.

PHOTO CREDITS

i. Arny Freytag; ii. Arny Freytag; 2. Larry Logan; 3. Yosef Karsh; 4. Elayne Lodge; 6. Elayne Lodge; 7. Elayne Lodge; 9. Elayne Lodge; 10. Arny Freytag; 11. Courtesy of Holly Madison; 12. Courtesy of Holly Madison; 13. James Trevenen; 14. Kenneth Johansson; 15. Playboy Enterprises; 16. Elayne Lodge; 17. Courtesy of Holly Madison; 20. Arny Freytag; 21. Playboy Enterprises; 24. Arny Freytag; 25. Courtesy of Bridget Marquardt; 26. Elayne Lodge; 27. Elayne Lodge; 29. Elayne Lodge; 31. Left photo by Elayne Lodge; right photo courtesy of Bridget Marquardt; 32. Arny Freytag; 34. Elayne Lodge; 36. Arny Freytag; 37. Courtesy of Kendra Wilkinson; 38. Courtesy of Kendra Wilkinson; 39. Elayne Lodge; 40. Kenneth Johansson; 42. Kenneth Johansson; 43. Courtesy of Kendra Wilkinson; 44. Elayne Lodge; 45. Arny Freytag; 46. Kenneth Johansson; 48. Kenneth Johansson; 51. Elayne Lodge; 53. Kenneth Johansson; 54. James Trevenen; 57. Jacob & Company; 58. Arny Freytag; 59. Arny Freytag; 60. Elayne Lodge; 61. Kenneth Johansson; 62. Elayne Lodge; 63. Bottom right photo by Bryant Horowitz; other photos by Elayne Lodge; 64. Bryant Horowitz & Julian Brown; 65. Arny Freytag; 66. Top photo by Kenneth Johansson; bottom photo by Elayne Lodge; 67. Playboy Enterprises; 68. Kenneth Johansson; 69. © 2005 Twentieth Century Fox Film Corporation and Alta Loma Entertainment, Inc. All rights reserved; 70. Kenneth Johansson; 71. Kenneth Johansson; 72. Left photo by Kea Wells & Carlena Bryant; other photos by Elayne Lodge; 73. Kenneth Johansson; 74. Larry Logan; 76. Larry Logan; 78. Larry Logan; 80. Larry Logan; 82. Larry Logan; 84. Larry Logan; 85. Larry

Logan; 86. Elayne Lodge; 87. Elayne Lodge; 88. Elayne Lodge; 89. Elayne Lodge; 90. Elayne Lodge; 91. Bottom photo by Arny Freytag; other photos by Elayne Lodge; 93. Elayne Lodge; 94. Elayne Lodge; 95. Elayne Lodge; 96. Kenneth Johansson; 97. Kenneth Johansson; 98. Elayne Lodge; 99. Top photo by Elayne Lodge; bottom photo by Kenneth Johansson; 100. Elayne Lodge; 102. Elayne Lodge; 103. Top photo by Elayne Lodge; bottom photo by Kenneth Johansson; 104. Elayne Lodge; 105. Elayne Lodge; 106. Elayne Lodge; 107. Elayne Lodge; 110. Elayne Lodge; 112. Elayne Lodge; 113. Elayne Lodge; 115. Kenneth Johansson; 117. Elayne Lodge; 118. Elayne Lodge; 119. Top right photo by Peter Iovino; other photos by Elayne Lodge; 120. Left photo by Elayne Lodge; right photo by Ruth Cruz; 121. Playboy Enterprises; drawing by Holly Madison; 122. Left photo by Elayne Lodge; right photo © 2006 Twentieth Century Fox Film Corporation and Alta Loma Entertainment, Inc. All rights reserved; 123. Elayne Lodge; 124. Elayne Lodge; 125. James Trevenen; 126. James Trevenen; 127. Elayne Lodge; 128. David Klein; 129. Left photos by Elayne Lodge; right photos by Kenneth Johansson; 130. Elayne Lodge; 131. Elayne Lodge; 132. Left photo by Jennifer Wilson; both photos © 2006 Twentieth Century Fox Film Corporation and Alta Loma Entertainment, Inc. All rights reserved; 133. Elayne Lodge; 134. David Klein; 136. Elayne Lodge; 138. Elayne Lodge; 140. Courtesy of Bridget Marquardt; 142. © 2005 Twentieth Century Fox Film Corporation and Alta Loma Entertainment, Inc. All rights reserved; 143. Elayne Lodge; 144. Elayne Lodge; 146. Top left and bottom right photos by Mickey Pierson; top right and bottom left photos by Elayne Lodge; 147. Elayne Lodge; 148. Elayne Lodge; 149. Top photo by David Klein; bottom photo © 2007 Twentieth Century Fox Film Corporation and Alta Loma Entertainment, Inc. All rights reserved; 150. Arny Freytag; 151. © 2007 Twentieth Century Fox Film Corporation and Alta Loma Entertainment, Inc. All rights reserved; 152. Top photo by Mickey Pierson; bottom photo by Elayne Lodge; 153. Elayne Lodge; 154. © 2007 Twentieth Century Fox Film Corporation and Alta Loma Entertainment, Inc. All rights reserved; 155. © 2007 Twentieth Century Fox Film Corporation and Alta Loma Entertainment, Inc. All rights reserved; 156. Elayne Lodge; 157. Elayne Lodge; 158. Left photo © 2007 Twentieth Century Fox Film Corporation and Alta Loma Entertainment, Inc. All rights reserved; right photo by Elayne Lodge; 159. Elayne Lodge; 160. David Klein; 161. Elayne Lodge; 162. Elayne Lodge; 164. Elayne Lodge; 165. Elayne Lodge; 166. Elayne Lodge; 167. Kenneth Johansson; 169. Elayne Lodge; 170. Bikini photo by Kenneth Johansson; other photos by Elayne Lodge; 171. Elayne Lodge; 172. Elayne Lodge; 173. Top left photo by David Klein; top center photo by Bryant Horowitz & Julian Brown; other photos by Elayne Lodge; 174. Top left photo by David Klein; top right photo © 2007 Twentieth Century Fox Film Corporation and Alta Loma Entertainment, Inc. All rights reserved; bottom right photo by Elayne Lodge; bottom left photo by Arny Freytag; 175. Kenneth Johansson; 176. Top photo by Elayne Lodge; center photo by Bryant Horowitz; bottom photo by Kenneth Johansson; 177. Arny Freytag; 178. Left photos by Elayne Lodge; right photo by Kenneth Johansson; 179. © 2007 Twentieth Century Fox Film Corporation and Alta Loma Entertainment, Inc. All rights reserved; 180. © 2007 Twentieth Century Fox Film Corporation and Alta Loma Entertainment, Inc. All rights reserved; 181. Elayne Lodge; 182. Left photo by Kenneth Johansson; other photos by Elayne Lodge; 183. James Trevenen; 184. © 2007 Twentieth Century Fox Film Corporation and Alta Loma Entertainment, Inc. All rights reserved; 185. Bottom right photo by Charles M. Gallyon; other photos by Elayne Lodge; 186. © 2007 Twentieth Century Fox Film Corporation and Alta Loma Entertainment, Inc. All rights reserved; 187. © 2007 Twentieth Century Fox Film Corporation and Alta Loma Entertainment, Inc. All rights reserved; 188. Elayne Lodge; 189. Elayne Lodge; 192. Elayne Lodge; 194. Kenneth Johansson; 196. Elayne Lodge; 197. Elayne Lodge; 198. Elayne Lodge; 200. Kenneth Johansson; 201. Kenneth Johansson; 202. Kenneth Johansson; 203. Kenneth Johansson; 204. James Trevenen; 206. James Trevenen; 207. James Trevenen; 208. James Trevenen; 210. © 2007 Twentieth Century Fox Film Corporation and Alta Loma Entertainment, Inc. All rights reserved; 211. Top photo © 2007 Twentieth Century Fox Film Corporation and Alta Loma Entertainment, Inc. All rights reserved; bottom photo by Carlena Bryant; 212. Right photo © 2007 Twentieth Century Fox Film Corporation and Alta Loma Entertainment, Inc. All rights reserved; left photo by Elayne Lodge; 213. Elayne Lodge; 214. Elayne Lodge; 216. Elayne Lodge; 217. David Klein; 218. David Klein; 219. David Klein; 220. Elayne Lodge; 222. Elayne Lodge; 224. Kenneth Johansson; 225. Courtesy of Bridget Marquardt; 226. Elayne Lodge; 227. Elayne Lodge; 228. Top photo by Ken Wells; bottom photo by Elayne Lodge; 229. Elayne Lodge; 230. Elayne Lodge; 231. Laurie Rodgers; 233. Elayne Lodge; 235. Elayne Lodge; 238. Elayne Lodge; 241. James Trevenen; 243. James Trevenen; 244. Elayne Lodge; 245. Elayne Lodge